WITHDRAWAL

The Supportive School

The Supportive School:
Wellbeing and the Young Adolescent

By

John Gray, Maurice Galton, Colleen McLaughlin, Barbie Clarke and Jennifer Symonds

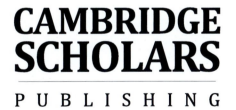

The Supportive School: Wellbeing and the Young Adolescent,
by John Gray, Maurice Galton, Colleen McLaughlin, Barbie Clarke and Jenny Symonds

This book first published 2011

Cambridge Scholars Publishing

12 Back Chapman Street, Newcastle upon Tyne, NE6 2XX, UK

British Library Cataloguing in Publication Data
A catalogue record for this book is available from the British Library

ISBN (10): 1-4438-3209-X, ISBN (13): 978-1-4438-3209-0

TABLE OF CONTENTS

LIST OF FIGURES AND TABLES

Figures

Tables

ACKNOWLEDGEMENTS

The authors would particularly like to thank the Nuffield Foundation which supported the research reported here through their Changing Adolescence research programme, chaired by Professor Sir Michael Rutter. This programme brought together a number of research teams from across the country to explore different aspects of adolescents' experiences as well as the factors influencing their development. We are especially grateful to the programme's Co-ordinator, Dr. Ann Hagell, for her thoughtful, critical and sympathetic support throughout our enquiries. Further information about this initiative can be found at the back of this volume.

Our thanks are also due to a number of other persons including: Professor Candace Currie of Edinburgh University who directed the collection of the international data from the Health Behaviour in School-aged Children surveys described in Chapters 6 and 8; Professor Jacquelynne Eccles of the University of Michigan for making data available from the Michigan Study of Adolescent Life Transitions; the librarians in the Faculty of Education at Cambridge University who facilitated the literature searches; and the anonymous referees who commented on an earlier draft.

A book such as this is the product of a team effort for which all share responsibility. However, the three directors of the research were particularly fortunate in having two Research Associates in the team who undertook much of the essential groundwork, tracking down references and undertaking initial analyses; I should particularly like to draw attention to their contributions to Chapters 4 (BC) and 5 (JS). Thanks too to Ewa Illakowicz who worked untiringly on the manuscript.

Finally, we are in debt to the very large number of researchers across the world (given the scale of our enterprise too many to thank individually by name) whose insights and publications have helped us to frame our own thinking. Whilst we ourselves take full responsibility for the interpretations of their research offered here, our own work is underpinned by theirs.

John Gray
Cambridge
July 2011

ABOUT THE AUTHORS

The authors of this book are (or were) members of the Faculty of Education at Cambridge University.

Professor John Gray is Professor of Education and a Fellow of the British Academy; he is well known internationally for his research into factors affecting school improvement.

Professor Maurice Galton is an Emeritus Professor and one of the UK's leading researchers on primary education and the transition from primary to secondary school.

Dr. Colleen McLaughlin is Deputy Head of the Faculty of Education and a widely respected authority on issues affecting young people's social and emotional development.

Dr. Barbie Clarke worked as a Research Associate on the project and now runs the Family, Kids and Youth consultancy.

Dr. Jennifer Symonds also worked as a Research Associate on the project and is now undertaking post-doctoral research in the USA and Finland.

CHAPTER ONE

INTRODUCTION

There is a widespread perception that the social and emotional wellbeing of young people has been in decline and that various problem behaviours are on the rise. Because children spend so much of their time in educational institutions, schools are assumed to be part of the problem and consequently many of those who wish to improve matters propose 'educational' solutions. The Labour government's *Every Child Matters* legislation (DfES, 2003) imposed 'a duty of wellbeing' on schools. Schools were to be held accountable for their students in five areas – 'being healthy', 'staying safe', 'enjoying and achieving', 'making a positive contribution' and 'achieving economic wellbeing'. In its wake a variety of interventions designed to improve young people's wellbeing have proliferated. Indeed, in the not so distant future, Ofsted has proposed that schools should be judged on their contributions to this aspect of performance as well as to their students' academic results.

We share the belief that educational institutions play an important role in structuring young people's identities and academic performance; there is a substantial body of research over many years to support this position. We are less certain, however, what contributions schooling (and crucially variations in the quality and experience of schooling) make to adolescents' mental health outcomes. This is largely a matter of omission. Research on educational outcomes has been pretty lop-sided. We know a good deal about the various factors which influence young people's cognitive achievement, much less about how these and other influences impact on their social and emotional development. However, there has also been a taken-for-grantedness about much of the research which does exist – of course schools 'make a difference'. One of our major concerns, therefore, has been to provide a firmer, research-based assessment of the school's contribution to adolescent wellbeing.

The research evidence that there have been significant changes in young people's *behaviour* over time is reasonably well-documented. More than a decade has passed since Rutter and Smith (1995) brought together studies showing that there have been upward trends in 'problem' behaviours amongst young people over the last half century. Collishaw and colleagues (2004) have added to this evidence more recently, demonstrating increases over some thirty years in relation to both conduct *and* emotional problems. Changes in family structure, peer groups, neighbourhood and youth cultures have been variously implicated as possible sources of these changes.

The Place of School in Young People's Lives

School undoubtedly features prominently in young people's perceptions of their own wellbeing. During 2005 *The Good Childhood Inquiry* surveyed around 8,000 14-16 year olds from across the UK (Pople, 2009: 17-18). The survey reports that children often 'spontaneously mentioned' school and education when asked about 'the ingredients of a good life'. The Inquiry found that what they liked most about school were the opportunities it provided to spend time with friends from whom they derived 'intimacy, support and pleasure'; the absence of such friendships was felt keenly by a minority. Good experiences of school were associated with having 'good teachers' who were 'kind and supportive,' 'passionate about their subjects' and who made lessons 'interesting and fun'. Young people liked being able to 'direct their own learning' and to learn by doing rather than just listening'. Some were 'enthusiastic about, or wanted to improve, their school buildings and facilities' whilst others were 'more concerned that the school environment should be supportive, respectful and friendly'. They were, in addition, concerned about bullying and the 'disruptive behaviour of other pupils'. Exams and schoolwork were also a source of stress.

Similar themes emerge from more qualitatively-oriented studies, particularly in relation to teachers. Rudduck and Flutter (2004: 76), for example, report that, in young people's view, 'good teachers' were crucial to their development as learners. Such teachers were 'human, accessible and reliable/consistent', 'respectful' of them and 'sensitive to their difficulties in learning', 'enthusiastic and positive' as well as being 'professionally skilled and expert in their subject'. Friendships were also important as sources of both social and academic support.

Methods and Scope

We take up many of these concerns in the chapters which follow but concentrate specifically on the educational components of these various debates. In the process we consider or touch on somewhere over 300 research reports of one kind or another. These were identified through a literature search which entered various terms into the major bibliographic search engines. We paid particular attention to those aspects of social and emotional development which have been linked to schooling. Our review turned up papers in psychology, health, medicine and criminology as well as education. We found that much of the research stemmed from the UK and the USA with further contributions, for the most part, from Scandinavia and Australia and New Zealand. We confined our attention, in the main, to studies of young adolescents in the 10-14 age-range although we did not exclude research which dealt with slightly older (or younger) persons.

We also looked for major surveys which lent themselves to analysis and reanalysis. We found a number of studies in the area of transfer from primary to secondary school which allowed us to undertake a meta-analysis. In many cases, however, the methods adopted by different researchers were not sufficiently comparable to make such approaches productive. However, amongst those we did identify, the World Health Organisation's Health Behaviour in School-aged Children (HBSC) was probably the most useful (see Currie *et al*, 2008 for an up-to-date account). A fuller account of our approach is available in Appendix 1.

The Challenges

We start by reviewing the incidence of social and emotional problems amongst young people before considering some aspects of the policy context. We then move on to consider research on the school's specific contribution to wellbeing and mental health outcomes. In the process we make more explicit a series of assumptions about what we term 'the supportive school'. We then turn to the literature on the effects of transfer from primary to secondary school on young people's development; this is just one of a variety of transitions which young people have to negotiate but undoubtedly an important one. We consider the findings of the very limited number of studies of school effectiveness which have strayed beyond measures of academic results. And we also explore the implications of various educational practices for 'less resilient' pupils. We end our review by examining changes in educational practice over the course of the last three or more decades and seek to place the English experience within the broader context of international practice. But first we consider briefly what the term 'wellbeing' might mean.

CHAPTER TWO

THE ASSESSMENT OF YOUNG PEOPLE'S WELLBEING

Both mental and social capital matter. But what mental health outcomes might one reasonably anticipate that schools might affect? As far as we have been able to establish, there is little consensus on this matter. Consequently, for the purposes of this book we have ranged quite widely in our pursuit of suitable measures –both of a more objective kind but also of a more subjective nature.

Measurement Issues

Broadly speaking, the research on 'wellbeing' we have considered falls into two categories. One group of studies consider what might be termed 'problem' cases, often informed by medical and psychiatric diagnoses although sometimes employing parental ratings as well. These studies use fairly tight definitions of adolescent conditions and behaviours. Resulting estimates of the proportions of the school population who are affected tend to be relatively small (typically below ten per cent). Whilst these studies sometimes touch on educational issues, their concern with schools as institutions is usually rather restricted.

Another group of studies use much broader measures with a view to tapping into adolescents' attitudes, dispositions, self-esteem and frames of mind. These studies also tend to produce much higher estimates of the proportions of the school population with particular conditions. This kind of research is typically more concerned with the social and emotional structures of individuals and organisations as measured through their self-reports. It is, of course, dependent on participants' attitudes and perceptions and the limitations of this kind of research are reasonably well-known. We have not, for example, found research within this tradition particularly suited to explaining the incidence of what might be termed more 'serious' mental health conditions.

The vast majority of the studies considered in this review draw upon this latter tradition of exploring attitudes, dispositions, self-esteem and frames of mind. Typically conducted by researchers with different orientations to those in the first group (who tend to be more medically inclined) they often employ different procedures to measure the same sorts of concepts. Individual researchers may employ similar measures over periods of time (such as the transition from primary to secondary school) but this does not necessarily seem to mean that other researchers, working in the same field, will use strictly comparable measures. This can make rigorous comparisons difficult to draw. And regrettably, at least from the stance of this,research, it is almost impossible to produce direct inferences across the two groups of studies. We may conjecture that pupils who report attitudinal problems probably have emotional and behavioural problems as well, which could be picked up by an external assessor using some sort of standardised rating procedure. Unfortunately, such connections, for logistical reasons amongst others, have rarely been made.

This tension between the two groups of studies is evident in the following discussion of the incidence of mental health outcomes.

The incidence of emotional and behavioural problems

In this chapter we attempt to provide a feel for the incidence of problems and conditions affecting adolescents that researchers have considered, particularly as they relate to education. In doing so we highlight the two contrasting traditions referred to above. Early adolescence is a period of 'transition' and exploration. For a minority it may be a period of 'turbulence' although most just experience this as a phase. 'Resilient' pupils can probably survive the majority of events, destabilising processes and some level of organisational dysfunction; less 'resilient' pupils are likely to be more vulnerable. How large is this latter group?

As part of the research for the Changing Adolescence Programme (see appendices), Collishaw and colleagues (2004) used national data-sets to track the growth in 'conduct disorders' over time (see Figure 1 below). Their measures were largely based on adults' assessments (including crucially parents) of young people's emotions and behaviour. The researchers report that 'conduct problems showed a continuous rise for both boys and girls aged 15-16 over the whole 25-year period (covered by the research)' although, as the figure shows, this seems to have plateaued at the most recent time-point. They comment that the rises seem to be largely attributable to increases 'in non-aggressive conduct problems such as lying, stealing and disobedience'.

Figure 1: Trends in Conduct Disorders

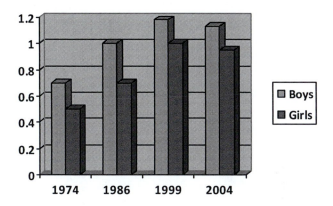

Source: Collishaw et al (2004)

The same authors also note increases on the emotional front (see Figure 2). They indicate that 'adolescent emotional problems (such as depression and anxiety) have increased for both girls and boys since the mid-1980s'. However, subsequent research has suggested that there was no further increase in problems after 1999 (Nuffield Foundation, 2009).

Figure 2: Trends in Emotional Problems

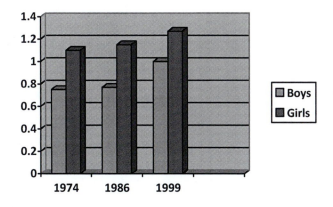

Source: Collishaw et al (2004)

A major study conducted by the Office for National Statistics (Perry-Langdon, 2004) provides further evidence of the current position (see Figure 3).

Figure 3: Incidence of Mental Disorders Amongst 11-15 Year Olds

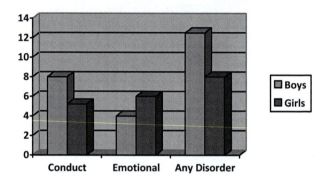

Source: Perry-Langdon (2004)

This research collected information from multiple informants (including, parents, teachers and children) and, in addition, employed some 'clinical input' to interpret the survey data. Amongst 11-15 year olds it reports that about one in eight boys and one in twelve girls had some form of 'mental disorder' (see Figure 3). As in the Collishaw study, boys were somewhat more likely to have conduct problems whilst girls tended have more emotional problems although we would note, in passing, that the two are likely, in many cases, to be connected – conduct disorders can lead to emotional problems and vice-versa. These estimates were not dissimilar from those identified in an earlier study, conducted by Melzer et al (1999), which also suggested that ten per cent of girls and 13 per cent of boys had some emotional disorder, a clinically significant conduct disorder or evidence of hyperactivity or other related syndromes.

A follow-up study of the same cohort three years later provides some insights into how far these 'disorders' persisted over time (Parry-Langdon, 2008). The evidence suggests those who had an emotional disorder at Time 1 were also more likely to be assessed as having an emotional disorder at Time 2. At the same time 58% of those with a conduct disorder at Time 1 were also reported to have a conduct disorder at Time 2. Children with special educational needs were twice as likely to have a conduct disorder as others. However, it is also clear from these estimates that young people change over this period – 60% of those with emotional disorders and 42% of those with conduct disorders were judged not to have them at the time of a follow-up three years later (see Table 1).

Table 1: Persistence of mental and other disorders amongst 11-13 year olds three years later

Nature of Disorder	Persistent (%)	Non-Persistent (%)
Emotional	40	60
Conduct	58	42
Hyperkinetic	23	9
Less Common	17	8
Any Mental Disorder	59	41

Source: Parry-Langdon (2008), Table 4.2.

A study of a large sample of young people attending schools in the socially deprived area of East London indicated higher levels of problems than some of the national estimates reported above suggest (Institute of Community Health Sciences, 2003). These researchers used several instruments Goodman's (1994) Strengths and Difficulties questionnaire which assesses hyperactivity, emotional problems, conduct problems, peer problems and pro-social behaviour; Rosenberg's (1989) Self-Esteem scale; Angold's (1987) Short Moods and Feelings Questionnaire which is used for rapid assessments of core depression symptomatology; and Zimet's (1988) Multi-Dimensional Scale of Perceived Social Support which addresses the perceived adequacy of 'social support' from family, friends and significant others. They report higher levels of 'psychological distress' in East London than elsewhere, especially amongst girls as well as lower levels of self-reported health.

Other measures used by researchers draw upon a wide range of psychological constructs to assess more specific aspects of young people's wellbeing. These include some whose reliability and validity have become quite well-established in the psychological literature but others which have been more *ad hoc* and tailored to specific research studies. Concepts covered elsewhere in this book include: academic self-concept; social adaptation; motivation; school-based anxiety; self-esteem; and attitudes to school and subjects such as English, Maths and Science.

In sum, there is evidence that the incidence of conduct disorders and emotional problems has been increasing and that these typically affect around ten per cent (and sometimes more) of the adolescent population. There is also a gendered component to young people's experiences and some increase in incidence as they get older. For many emotional and conduct problems are of a relatively temporary nature and do not seem to persist; for a significant minority of young people, however, these and other disorders are more enduring.

'Life Satisfaction' and More Holistic Measures

Several studies have employed global or holistic measures of young people's wellbeing. The Health Behaviour in School-Aged Children (HBSC) study provides an example; it is a major survey of the health and mental condition of young people in numerous countries supported by the World Health Organisation (Currie et al, 2008) and it has incorporated a range of self-report measures.

Amongst these measures is the concept of 'life satisfaction', a relatively global measure of a young person's 'wellbeing'. The study argues that 'life satisfaction' can be defined as 'a person's evaluation of various areas of his or her life' (Currie, 2008: 63). Young people were asked to rate their own life satisfaction using a measurement technique called the Cantril Ladder on which there are ten steps ranging from 'the best possible life' to 'the worst possible life'. The researchers argue that 'life satisfaction (was) associated with a host of health-related outcomes' including substance use and physical activity. Crucially, for this review, they suggest that higher levels of life satisfaction are associated with 'positive school experience' whilst 'a negative experience of school is related to lower life satisfaction'.

Figure 4 shows the results for English adolescents. It is based on a series of cross-sectional surveys and consequently we cannot be completely confident that the emerging patterns relate to individual trajectories. Bearing this caveat in mind, however, the evidence does seem to suggest that whilst 'life satisfaction' remained pretty high amongst English adolescent boys as they got older, this was not true to the same extent for girls; the responses of the older groups were considerably lower than those of the 11 year olds, especially around the age of 13.

Figure 4: Incidence of Positive 'Life Satisfaction' Amongst English Adolescents in 2005/06

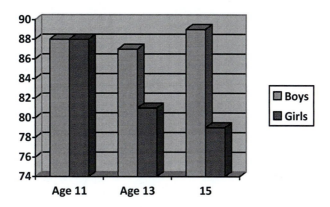

Source: Currie et al (2008)

The figure does not show the proportions of young people experiencing less than positive life satisfaction (scores below six) but clearly these proportions can be inferred from the evidence. Around one in eight boys might be in this position. The figures for girls (especially those aged 15) are considerably higher with around one in five saying they were affected. The position of English teenagers was very similar to that of young people across the international samples (not shown). Nonetheless, we should perhaps note that in *The Good Childhood Inquiry* around a quarter (27%) of the 8,000 young people sampled agreed with the statement that 'I often feel depressed' (Pople, 2009).

Whether a young person 'likes school' or not is another global measure employed by the HBSC researchers. They argue that 'school satisfaction has been considered as an indicator of the emotional aspect of quality of life in the school setting' (Currie et al, 2008: 41). Young people were asked how they felt about school with response options ranging from 'like it a lot' to 'don't like it at all'. The researchers suggest that 'a positive experience of school is seen as a resource for health whilst a negative experience may constitute a risk factor'. In addition, 'liking school', they report, may help 'to protect against sexual risk-taking, substance use and smoking'. Conversely students who dislike school are 'those most likely to be failing academically and to be at greatest risk of dropping out, adopting unhealthy behaviours, exhibiting psychosomatic symptoms and experiencing reduced quality of life'.

In sum, using global measures such as these, the greater majority of 11-15 year olds would appear to be positive, both about their lives and, in the main, their schooling. However, as we shall subsequently show, the evidence also suggests that there can be significant changes on some of these measures during adolescence.

Conclusions

The idea of adolescent 'wellbeing' is not well-defined in the studies we have considered. A small minority of studies have used well-established, valid and reliable measures whose strengths (and weaknesses) have been become known over a period of time. Such studies, however, have been largely concerned with establishing the general contours of school populations. They have not necessarily had much to say about those aspects of schooling which have helped to shape young people's responses. The much larger group of studies reviewed in the following pages have employed a more eclectic approach: sometimes they have employed well-established instruments but, more frequently, they have drawn on a range of different measures whose links with each other are not necessarily well understood.

Researchers have ranged widely in pursuit of measures of adolescents' wellbeing. Bringing the estimates from the various sources described above together, one can begin to discern some patterns. In broad terms whilst the greater majority of young people report positive mental health outcomes, up to one in ten (or, depending on the measure sometimes more) seem to encounter difficulties. Boys are reported to have more conduct disorders than girls whilst girls appear to have more emotional problems than their male counterparts. Between the ages of 11 and 15 the proportions of adolescents encountering difficulties also seems to rise steadily (although not dramatically). For roughly half of those experiencing difficulties, however, the position seems to be a temporary one; their conditions subsequently become somewhat alleviated.

CHAPTER THREE

THE CHANGING POLICY CONTEXT

Richard Layard has argued that 'if mental health difficulties have increased, it must be because the quality of children's experience has deteriorated' (Layard, 2009: 11). He did not refer explicitly to schooling but, in the context of this review, the inference must be that some aspects of their educational experiences have taken a turn for the worse. Establishing what precisely has changed, however, is a more difficult matter and solid evidence is frequently lacking. We consider three key questions here. First, whether there have been structural changes in the organisation of schooling which might have affected wellbeing issues. Then we consider the under-explored role of the school in relation to these same concerns. Finally, we draw upon some international evidence relating to comparisons across educational systems.

The changing nature of school organisation

The 1988 Education Reform Act is often seen as a turning point in the second half of the 20th century. It introduced a series of reforms including the development of a National Curriculum, accompanied by a programme of national testing and assessment, that involved all pupils, as well as a series of initiatives whose major purpose was to increase competition between schools and facilitate parental choice.

Since that time performance levels have risen, at least in terms of the traditional hurdle of the proportions achieving five or more A*-C grades in GCSE examinations (Croxford et al, 2006). Rising attainment levels might be expected to be accompanied by increased feelings of wellbeing. But social inequalities have remained fairly constant at the same time which may have produced a countervailing tendency (Raffe et al, 2006).

One needs to be careful in assuming that change has occurred simply because it has been mandated. Some features of the educational scene have remained relatively constant despite concerted efforts to change them – the school curriculum, for example, has barely altered (Chitty, 2002) and teaching methods have largely resisted change. Schools may, however, be spending more time on those parts of the curriculum (such as literacy and numeracy) which are formally assessed. There has also been some resurgence in direct instruction, despite the evidence that pupils, particularly those with anti-learning dispositions, prefer to work collaboratively in smaller groups and other more independent ways (Pell et al, 2007).

Structural changes to the educational system have had other far-reaching consequences. Moves towards comprehensive education, for example, opened up opportunities for larger groups of young people to participate in the public examination system but they also increased the pressure on those who were not in a position to climb over the various competitive hurdles placed in their way (Gray, 2005). However, as Rutter and Maughan (2002: 469) have observed, 'despite sweeping changes in the educational system, we lack good empirical evidence of the pros and cons of selective versus non-selective systems'. What was true in 2002 remains the case today; furthermore, as far as we are aware, there are no plans in place to conduct this kind of study.

There are other significant areas of school organisation where we lack good evidence over time,. Amongst the areas where research is largely missing are the effects of school intakes, of schools' approaches to ability grouping and of their deployment of resources. We are aware of the extent to which there have been reforms in all three areas over the last two decades but such little research as exists is largely silent on the impact of these important developments on pupils' wellbeing.

It is difficult to predict what the effects these various changes might have – it is conceivable that they have mostly cancelled each other out. However, there are two developments which, it could be argued, have had more direct implications for wellbeing. The first relates to aspects of motivation. Young people may have adapted to the changing pressures on them by becoming more instrumental in their attitudes. Awareness of the longer-term consequences of high-stakes assessment has also heightened. The second concerns the extent to which schools and teachers have become more conscious of the need to pay attention to issues of motivation and wellbeing. They have invested heavily in ensuring that the various processes of transfer operate more smoothly. However, many of these interventions have been relatively short-term and often more focused on organisational arrangements than on young people's emotional and social pathways into secondary schooling.

Many of the concerns addressed here have historically been the preserve of schools' pastoral care systems. During the 1970s and 1980s pastoral care was an area of growth and development in secondary schools, its trajectory fuelled by the development of comprehensive schooling. Various authors advocated its promotion (Blackburn, 1975; Hamblin, 1978). They were concerned that educational provision took a 'personal' rather than 'technical' approach (Lefstein, 2005). As Power (1996: 3) has argued there was an 'implicit, and sometimes explicit, belief that pastoral care (could) counteract some of the apparently undesirable effects of the academic dimension'. But there were also concerns that pastoral systems were being used for the purposes of social control (Best el al, 1983; Lang and Marland, 1986). Surprisingly little of the thinking that underpinned pastoral care systems, however, was research-based.

Since that period the notion of pastoral care *provided by teachers* has come under considerable pressure. Many schools now employ people other than teachers to undertake work within the pastoral domain previously performed by teachers. There are advantages to having specialists in such roles but also problems. In the process the status of this work within schools has suffered. There has also been a change in the focus of activities along with the nomenclature. Mentoring, for example, is often targeted not so much at those who have emotional needs as at those who are identified as being in a position to raise their attainment in public exams whilst Heads of Year/House have often been retitled as Curriculum Co-ordinators. Out of school provision for pupils who have been excluded or have attendance problems has also grown. In short, it can no longer be assumed that schools have well-developed pastoral systems in place.

There seem to be two major reasons for this state of affairs. First, and importantly, the concept of pastoral care has gone into decline. It has been replaced by other terminology – 'healthy schools', 'wellbeing' and so on. But second, and just as significantly, roles in schools have changed as a result of initiatives undertaken as part of the government's Workforce Reform. As a generalisation, school services have become both more specialised and, increasingly, focused on academic outcomes. Form tutors survive in most schools but in many a division of labour has been developed whereby teachers are engaged primarily in teaching whilst support staff play a major role in managing those who are 'vulnerable' such as pupils with special needs or emotional and behavioural difficulties. As an Ofsted report (2004) underlined, such pupils tend to get tracked into out of school provision whose quality can be variable to say the least. Perhaps most worryingly, schools and local authorities are reported to be failing, in many instances, to track such pupils or to secure a comprehensive view of their whereabouts, achievements and destinations. These findings are underlined by a more recent study by Blatchford and colleagues (2009: 124) which reported some marginalisation of the care of pupils with emotional and behavioural difficulties in mainstream settings.

Crucially, support staff were reported to be providing 'alternative' rather than additional support'.

The under-explored role of the school

Responsibility for enhancing and promoting mental health in schools is acknowledged in policy documents and is enshrined in the United Kingdom in several policies, as well as being a topic of international research, policy making and focus (Department for Education and Skills, 2003; Department of Health, 2004). How widely this concern is acknowledged is, however, another matter. Schools vary in the extent to which they put such matters high on their agendas.

During 2008 Ofsted, the schools inspection agency, launched a consultation document on the school's 'contribution to wellbeing' (Ofsted, 2008). This attracted a series of headlines. *The Guardian* newspaper declared on its front page, for example, that 'schools may be judged on teenage pregnancy rates and drug problems' and that Ofsted had drawn up a plan to 'include 18 social targets in Ofsted reports' (30 April, 2008). These would include 'records of teenage pregnancy rates, pupils' drug problems, criminal records and obesity levels'. Needless to say the response was very mixed. The NAHT (one of the headteacher associations) said that it was 'concerned about the extent to which schools are held accountable for all the ills of society', adding that it had 'become quite ridiculous'. The ATL, another union, described the proposals as 'madness'. In short, the proposals appeared to have touched a raw nerve within the school system.

In fact, as Figure 5 below reveals, Ofsted has been grading schools in a general way on their wellbeing outcomes for some while. The graph shows the percentages of schools awarded each inspection grade. Their judgements suggest that in roughly 90% of primary schools learners' 'overall development and wellbeing' were 'good or better'. However, bearing in mind that hardly any schools at all were awarded the lowest grade (4), around ten per cent of primary and middle schools were on the borderline as were just under 30% of secondary schools.

There have been a number of government-sponsored initiatives to promote 'good practice' in personal, social and health education (PSHE) But, whilst establishing some evidence of progress and improved teaching over the previous five years, an Ofsted (2007b) evaluation was concerned at the extent to which teachers lacked training, relevant content knowledge and skills.

The Ofsted consultation document suggests some ambiguity about the role of the school in contributing to these outcomes. 'The extent to which schools can influence outcomes for their pupils', they remark, 'is variable' adding that it 'would not be disputed that schools make a demonstrable difference to their pupils' achievement'. But they also add that 'schools can have a direct and significant impact on elements of other *Every Child Matters* outcomes, for example the extent to which young people feel safe from bullying in school and their attendance rates'. The document went on to state that there was 'no intention to hold schools to account for wellbeing outcomes over which they have limited influence such as levels of child obesity or teenage pregnancy rates' before reiterating that 'what a school can reasonably be held accountable for is its contribution to improving outcomes and its impact'. What is missing from this account, however, is a clear view of precisely which wellbeing outcomes schools actually affect as well as how.

Figure 5: Ofsted gradings of schools in relation to 'overall development and wellbeing of the learners'

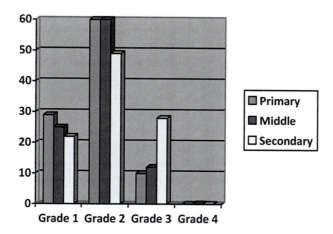

Source: Wyatt (2008)

Researchers have also given some consideration to the extent of variations between schools, although not, it should be said, on the same scale as Ofsted. Does the research support the view that some schools are better at fostering wellbeing outcomes than others? We shall consider some of the evidence in subsequent chapters.

International Comparisons

The possibility that England (and perhaps the United Kingdom more generally) may have some problems with respect to wellbeing issues was brought home forcibly in a recent international 'league table' published by UNICEF (2007). For the purposes of presentation Table 2 below is confined to the top and bottom countries in the survey. The report (2007: 3) presents a variable picture; it concluded that 'all countries have weaknesses that need to be addressed and no country features in the top third of the rankings for all six dimensions of child well-being (though the Netherlands and Sweden come close to doing so)'. But it also noted that 'the UK and the USA found themselves in the bottom third of the rankings for five of the six dimensions reviewed'. Indeed, on several measures, including 'subjective wellbeing', the UK occupied one of the bottom two places.

The subjective wellbeing measure (see Column 6 in Table 2) is of particular relevance to this discussion. It combined three items relating to health, school life and personal wellbeing although it is debatable how far such items can be grouped together. The index summated scores relating to the percentages of young people rating their own health no more than 'fair' or 'poor', the percentages of pupils 'liking school a lot', the percentages of pupils rating themselves above the mid-point of the Life Satisfaction scale (referred to in the previous section) and also reporting negatively about their personal wellbeing in relation to feeling 'like an outsider or left out', 'feeling awkward and out of place' and 'feeling lonely'. Again, England occupied the bottom place, suggesting that English adolescents faced a particularly serious set of problems by comparison with their counterparts elsewhere.

Table 2: The UNICEF League Table: top and bottom four countries in rank order out of 21

Country	Material Wellbeing	Health & Safety	Educational Wellbeing	Family & peer relationships	Behaviours & Risks	Subjective Wellbeing
Holland	10	2	6	3	3	1
Sweden	4	1	5	15	1	7
Denmark	4	4	8	9	6	12
Finland	3	3	4	17	7	11
Austria	8	20	19	16	16	4
Hungary	20	17	13	6	18	13
USA	17	21	12	20	20	-
UK	18	12	17	21	21	20

Source: UNICEF (2007).

The research team that produced the UNICEF league table has since updated their analyses (CPAG, 2009). Whilst the items used on this second occasion were of more recent origin, the UK still looked to have problems. In the 'subjective wellbeing domain it was placed 21st out of 28 countries. The researchers note that the Netherlands again did 'particularly well with children reporting high wellbeing in school' (CPAG, 2009: 4).

Conclusions

There have been a considerable number of reforms in the educational system over the last three decades. Whilst these changes may have had consequences for wellbeing issues, few of them have been launched with wellbeing specifically in mind. Furthermore, it is almost impossible to say what their longer-term effects have been. Amongst the important questions that it is difficult to answer with any degree of certainty with respect to wellbeing issues are the effects of school intakes and selective/non-selective systems; both, it seems reasonable to suppose, have had some impact.

In recent years a number of policy initiatives have sought to tackle wellbeing issues more directly. Ofsted gradings suggest that up to 30% of secondary schools may still have issues that need to be addressed and other research hints at quite substantial variations between schools in wellbeing outcomes. Indeed, the proportions may be higher. Again, however, comparative judgements over time are unlikely to be founded on well-conducted research.

The UK has not shown up well in international comparisons, especially in comparison with Nordic and Scandinavian countries. Its position varies a little depending on the indicator but on most of them its performance has languished in the lower reaches of the league tables. Reasons for this state of affairs are much debated and will be considered in greater detail later on.

CHAPTER FOUR

THE SUPPORTIVE SCHOOL

It will be clear from the previous discussion that we believe that schools can make some difference to their pupils' wellbeing. As Resnick (2005) has argued, schools should be involved in 'the intentional, deliberative process of providing support, relationships, experience and opportunities that promote positive outcomes for young people'. But which particular aspects of schooling matter most? In the sections that follow we identify several over-arching areas of activity and experience which the research we have reviewed suggests may be particularly influential in influencing young people's wellbeing.

Central to our discussion is the notion of **'school connectedness'**. This concept is of relatively recent provenance although its components are of much longer standing. As the US National Research Council (2003) put it: 'If students are to invest themselves in the forms of mastery required by schools, they must perceive the general enterprise of schooling as legitimate, deserving of their committed effort and honouring them as respected members'. 'School connectedness' provides a summary way of describing a nexus of such activities and experiences including relationships between peers and with teachers, levels of pupil satisfaction with what they are experiencing, feelings of membership of the 'learning community' and aspects of participation and student voice. Many of these areas have been researched in some detail over the years and ideas about their nature and salience are relatively well-developed.

By contrast, research into the structural and organisational aspects of schooling which relate to wellbeing is surprisingly under-represented in the research; most of the studies which we have reviewed have focused on their effects on cognitive outcomes. We have coined the phrase 'thinking small' to capture these elements of schools' functioning. Areas which are covered by this concept include: structural components of school organisation such as school and class size, pastoral elements related to such things as house systems and tutor groups, aspects of the processes of teaching and learning as well as the physical environment of schooling.

A third area of our research relates to the **process of transfer** from primary school and the ways in which schools help their pupils to adjust to the changing demands of secondary schooling. This transition coincides with early adolescence and is something about which young people worry quite a lot. But are there longer-lasting consequences? There is a strong tradition of research in this area and, as part of this review, we have explored a substantial number of empirical studies which have tracked aspects of pupils' development related to their well-being over longer periods of time. The majority of groups of young people make a successful transition but some appear to be more vulnerable at this point.

Finally, there are a number of other potential **points of stress** in the early stages of secondary schooling in addition to those related to transfer. Peer victimisation can be a particular problem for wellbeing whilst other vulnerable groups can also be identified at this point. How the school handles these 'at risk' students can have significant implications for a range of more serious outcomes which may eventually culminate in exclusion with major, potentially life-changing, consequences.

The elements described above have often been studied in isolation from each other. We have found this separation unhelpful in explaining wellbeing outcomes and, in the final part of this section, we argue that the concept of the **'supportive school'** can bring a degree of coherence to the discussions.

School Connectedness

The phrase 'school connectedness' has gained considerable currency in recent years. Other related terms which connote similar concerns include 'school engagement', 'school relatedness' and 'school belonging' whilst earlier work on school climate and school 'ethos' is also clearly pertinent.

In our review we identified five areas of research that were relevant to the notion of school connectedness. These included:

- relationships with a particular emphasis on those pertaining between young people and their teachers and also with and amongst their peers;
- levels of young people's 'satisfaction' with their experiences at school;
- young people's sense of membership of their school as a 'learning community' as well as the extent to which they participated in and exercised 'voice' in relation to their schools' affairs and activities;

- how schools have handled academic pressure and the stresses that are potentially associated with them; and
- the impact of 'thinking small' developments.

To have a sense of 'connectedness' with school, young people need to feel that they belong in some way to the school (Finn 1993, 1997). Pupils who feel connected to school, and feel cared for by people at school, report a higher degree of wellbeing (Resnick et al, 1997; Eccles et al, 1997; Steinberg, 1996; McNeely et al, 2002). The ability of a child to connect to school during adolescence has also been shown to be a key protective factor and one that lowers the likelihood of health-risk behaviour, while simultaneously enhancing positive educational outcomes (Resnick et al, 1993; Resnick, 2000; Glover et al, 1998; Blum and Libbey, 2004; Libbey, 2004).

Several factors are related to young adolescents' sense of motivation and achievement at school, including both parental support (Bowen and Bowen, 1998: Rosenfeld et al, 2000) and peer support (Rosenfeld et al, 2000). Early adolescents' engagement with school is instrumental to young people's social and cognitive development, leading to a sense of achievement and high self-esteem, but it is also fundamental to their wellbeing (Finn, 1993;Newmann, 1992; Marks 2000). Young adolescents who are disengaged from school and have poor relationships with peers and teachers are also likely to have a higher risk of displaying anxiety or depressive symptoms and are more likely to use drugs and to engage in socially disruptive behavior. They are, in addition, less likely to complete secondary school (Resnick et al, 1997; Bond et al, 2001 and 2004; Barclay and Doll, 2001; Doll and Hess, 2001; Marcus and Sanders-Reio, 2001; Catalano et al, 1996; Smith, 2006).

Whilst the majority of young people have a positive relationship with their school, a significant minority reports *not* having a sense of connectedness or engagement (Murray and Greenberg, 2000), although this is a complex picture and trends are difficult to ascertain. Roeser and colleagues (2000: 459) ask how well aspects of school ethos 'provide a fit with (young people's) implicit psychological needs for competence, autonomy and quality relationships with others?' In the studies that focus on pupils' perceptions the characteristics of the relationships that are seen as particularly important are related to: perceived support or caring; perceived fairness; respect, trust and being listened to; feelings of competence; engagement in decision making or agency; acting on the pupil's behalf or intervening; and being positive.

To what extent is 'school connectedness' related to the broader measure of 'life satisfaction' we discussed in Chapter 2? Thompson et al (2006) used HBSC data to explore relationships between school connectedness and other aspects of young people's lives. Greater connectedness was found amongst younger students, students in two-parent households, amongst those who performed well in school, who participated in many extra-curricular activities and those who had a large number of friends.

The HBSC surveys also provide some insights into the strength of these relationships. Both boys and girls who reported higher 'life satisfaction' scores were more likely to 'like school', perceive their 'peers as supportive' and believe their teachers thought they were doing well at school. They were also less likely to feel 'pressured by their schoolwork' (see Table 4.8, Ravens-Sieberer et al, 2004). However, whilst these relationships were all statistically significant they were not particularly strong – the correlations averaged around 0.2.

Relationships with teachers

It is a moot point whether, from a young person's perspective, relationships with teachers or relationships with peers are more important. Given that we are concerned here primarily with the ways in which schools influence wellbeing outcomes and the extent to which peer relationships take place both within and beyond the school boundaries, however, it seems reasonable to start first with teacher-pupil relationships.

There are two aspects of teacher-pupil relationships that are of particular interest. First, there are the relationships that individual teachers have with individual students; not surprisingly, students who have positive perceptions of their relationships with teachers tend to do better in a number of respects. Second, and perhaps as importantly, there are settings in which the staff group *as a body* attempts to nurture good relationships with students. It seems likely that students who find themselves in this latter situation are in a position to benefit doubly although most of the studies we review below do not make such a tight distinction.

Croll and Moses (2003) report that the majority of pupils like their teachers. 85% of those in Year 7 agreed with the statement 'I like most of my teachers' whilst 89% denied that their 'teachers (were) always getting at me'. These percentages largely held up in Year 8 but by Year 9 relationships appear to have dropped off. Only 69% of those in Year 9 'liked most of (their) teachers', for example, and the percentage reporting that teachers were not 'always getting' at them had fallen to 78%.

Why do relationships matter? The short answer is that they can affect academic outcomes as well as emotional wellbeing. Research also emphasizes the nexus of connections between matters of wellbeing, academic achievement and pupils' motivation and engagement. Emotional wellbeing is enhanced by academic achievement and good teaching, as academic achievement is dependent on 'an ability to meet social as well as academic challenges' (Wentzel, 1998: 202). Earlier research, particularly that by Rutter (1991) and Eccles and Midgley (1989), showed the impact of school success on later social development and these findings are reinforced in more recent research.

There is, nonetheless, a problem with much of the research we have considered on teacher relationships. It is often assumed that there is a causal mechanism at work – better relationships foster better outcomes for pupils. In reality, most studies either do not test this proposition or are not in a position to do so. A study by Reddy and colleagues (2003) is an exception to this broad generalisation. They found that 'students perceiving increasing teacher support showed corresponding decreases in depressive symptoms and increases in self-esteem'. Importantly, from the viewpoint of this review, they also tested 'a competing model' which 'gave additional support for pathways of influence *from* perceptions of teacher support to depression and self-esteem, rather than the reverse' (our emphasis).

Early research in the area of young people's 'resilience' identified the importance of both teacher-pupil *and* pupil-pupil relationships. It focused on the relationship between the adults in children's social worlds and the influences of (and interactions) with family, peers and other social organisations. As part of these investigations schools were identified as important sites in relation to mental health, and the academic as well as the psychosocial aspects of school were seen as very important to adolescents' healthy development (Howard et al, 1999).

Roeser and colleagues (2000: 458) studied mental health interventions in a number of US middle schools. They have argued that 'perhaps the best mental health intervention teachers can implement ... is good teaching' which, in turn, affects the complex dynamic between social, emotional and academic development at school. As they go on to argue, feeling academically competent and valuing school are 'two intra-psychic resources that may help youth with poor mental health overcome other life adversities that often threaten the attainment of a good education.' (*op. cit*: 457). Recent UK research (Mayall, 2007) is particularly helpful here because it has focused on specific elements of teacher-pupil relationships and has emphasised young adolescents' desire for positive pupil-teacher relationships. As Rudduck and Flutter (2004) have also argued, what was striking about teachers identified by young people as 'good' was that 'the qualities that mattered to pupils tended to be as much about how they were *treated* as how they were taught'.

The development of 'coping strategies' has been identified as a particularly significant factor in protecting young people psychosocially and helping to promote their wellbeing. Elements have included self-efficacy, the ability to self-reflect, self-reliance, maintaining a positive outlook and problem solving (Vostanis, 2007). Children's positive experiences of, and engagement in, secure relationships, educational attainment, and friendships have also been identified as important. These are clearly areas which teachers can influence.

The central place of relationships in facilitating wellbeing more generally has been acknowledged in reviews over the last decade (see, for example, Durlak and Wells, 1997). As Weare and Gray (2003: 56) suggest: '... the learning of emotional and social competence is centrally about learning to be a warm human being who can make worthwhile personal relationships with others. The ability to develop relationships is only likely to happen in contexts which are themselves based on and which foster warm personal relationships.'

There has been some European, some Australian and a larger body of American research to support this view. However, as with many aspects of this review, there is a need to be cautious about directly transferring findings from the USA and other contexts. Juvonen and colleagues (2004), for example, report that the international comparisons show that 'US middle-school students have negative perceptions of their learning conditions. Compared with their peers in other countries they reported the highest levels of emotional and physical problems, viewed the climate of their schools most negatively and considered the peer culture in school to be unkind and unsupportive'. On the other hand US students reported more favourably on levels of teacher support, parental involvement and 'the lack of perceived pressure to do well in school' (what the authors refer to as 'academic pressure'). We should note in passing, however, that the US middle school is a substantially larger institution than its UK counterpart.

Many of the factors that are related to success in school are also factors that play a part in shaping emotional wellbeing; this seems to be especially true amongst high achievers (Suldo and Huebner, 2006). Such things as persistence at tasks, having positive goals, feeling included in a social group and in a worthwhile enterprise, feelings of competence and safety, developing problem-solving capacities and having a sense of efficacy.

Motivation and success at school are, in turn, influenced by relationships with teachers. Indeed, a number of researchers have argued that teachers are absolutely central and play a particular part in the development and maintenance of emotional wellbeing (Wentzel 1998: Roeser et al, 2000; Weare and Gray, 2003). Wentzel, in particular, reports that social support from teachers is a key variable for all students, not just vulnerable or minority groups; however, she also warns against generalising to all age groups as she feels that, whilst all students probably need some support, US middle school students constitute a particular group with particular needs.

Relationships between social support, feelings of emotional wellbeing or distress, and teacher-pupil relationships have attracted further interest over the past decade. Roeser et al (2000: 458) have argued that the 'theoretical argument is straightforward' - 'to the extent that adolescents perceive teacher and school staff as providing them with opportunities to develop their academic and social competencies, to exercise autonomous control over aspects of their learning and to feel cared for and supported during learning, adolescents' perceptions of their academic competence, their valuing of school and their emotional well-being should all be enhanced.'

Levels of teacher support appear to be particularly important with respect to certain mental health outcomes although clearly, in this area, causal directions need to be handled with care. Studies have shown that students' *perceptions* of support are of central importance and that whether these perceptions correspond to actual levels of support is not the most important thing (Roeser et al, 2000). As Reddy and colleagues (2003: 122) have argued: 'it is not the support experiences themselves, but the cognitive representations of providers as available and supportive, that influence outcomes.'

Perceived teacher support also seems important in other ways, especially in relation to depression and self-esteem (Reddy et al, 2004; Roeser et al, 2000). McNeely and Falci (2004) suggest that it is particularly important in 'the initiation, escalation and reduction of participation in six adolescent health-risk behaviours'. Teacher support reliably predicted changes in psychological adjustment. 'In particular, students who perceived increasing levels of teacher support evidenced corresponding decreases in depression and increases in self-esteem. Likewise perceptions of decreasing teacher support corresponded with increases in depression and losses in self-esteem' (Reddy et al, 2003: 133). There were also links between perceived availability of teacher support and increased motivation to learn as well as better mental health over time (Roeser et al, 2000).

Many students feel that support from their teachers declines over time; this is perhaps to be expected as adolescents develop and get older. However, Reddy and colleagues (2003. 135) note that 'although these decrements may be explained in part by normal developmental changes, the less voluntary aspects of this loss of teacher support are cause for concern'. Harden and colleagues (2001: 147) also report concerns from young people about teachers not being a good source of emotional support or self-esteem. 'Young people identified few school-related facilitators of their mental health and relations with teachers tended to be described in negative terms.' They also reported a lack of consultation with young people on the barriers to and facilitators of mental health, although they had very clear views. Young people, for their part, identified three major aspects of school life as barriers or facilitators to their mental health: academic achievement and engagement in learning; boredom at school; and, critically for this part of the review, the ways their teachers behaved.

It should come as no surprise that relationships with teachers matter to young people. However, it is important to stress that the majority of adolescents in these various studies *did* feel supported by their teachers and felt that they were working in environments that supported meaningful learning, mastery and autonomy. Murray and Greenberg (2000), for example, found that two thirds of US 11-12 year olds reported 'good' or 'adequate' pro-social relationships with teachers. But, at the same time, there appear to be quite sizeable minorities of young people who do not seem to have shared these experiences and we shall turn our attention to them later on.

Relationships with teachers may also have longer term implications. Smith (2006: 4), in his study of youth transitions and crime in Edinburgh, offers a significant insight. He particularly emphasises the role of teacher-pupil relationships in attachment to school. 'Attachment to school', he found, was 'related to young people's behaviour more widely in school and more widely to delinquent and criminal conduct. Amongst these variables, the most important 'dimension was attachment to teachers, but the belief that school success will bring later reward was also important'. 'Attachment to teachers at age 13 was (also) related to lower levels of misbehaviour and delinquency at age 15'.

Not surprisingly, in view of these findings, Smith concluded that 'there is a role for schools in preventing the development of delinquent behaviour' (*op. cit*: 4). Other researchers have reached similar conclusions in relation to other aspects of young people's wellbeing. By focusing on relationships with teachers, educators could harness developmental processes, such as the search for and development of identity in early adolescents (Roeser et al, 2000), the need for emotional safety and the need to affiliate and belong in schools (Juvonen, 2007; Goodenow, 1993).

The question of gender differences in teacher support has not received much attention. Vieno et al (2004) looked at the relationships between teacher support aimed at 'fostering feelings in students of being listened to and understood' amongst a sample of young Italians. They concluded that 'if teacher support is crucial to boys' school satisfaction and achievement, boys' classmates also play a crucial role in helping them to cope with school-related stress' (2004: 230). But girls, they concluded, placed a greater emphasis on peer support than teacher support.

There is a further aspect of teacher-pupil relationships that seems to us important but which remains relatively under-explored. Most studies focus on such relationships in the round – that is between whole groups of pupils and school staff as a body of adults. Lightfoot (1983: 355), however, reports an important but significant nuance on this interpretation. Adolescents in US high schools, she suggests, 'tend to seek comfort not only by close affiliation with selected peers but also search out special adults with whom they form close relationships'. The 'high school experience', she argues, can be 'totally transformed by a vital relationship with a special adult'; conversely, young people who are unable to form such a relationship may be more vulnerable.

Much of the literature emphasises that it is the disaffected or disengaged young person that needs particular support from teachers. Suldo and Huebner (2006: 198) found 'that adolescents with extremely low and average life satisfaction reported similar levels of teacher support, but that especially high teacher support distinguished students with extremely high life satisfaction'. Our conclusion, however, aligns more closely with that of Roeser and colleagues (1998) – in short that the influence of teachers is potentially powerful for *all* pupils.

Relationships with peers

Young people form friendships both within and outside school – often such relationships are mutually reinforcing, sometimes they are not. The ability to form friends, especially in school, appears to have a direct effect on how children cope with crisis as well as their levels of wellbeing. Young people with an understanding of the emotional needs of others are able to form better and more intimate relationships (Dunn and Cutting, 1999; Dunn, 2004; Berndt, 1981; Douvan and Adelson, 1966).

Buhrmester's research (1990) is particularly interesting. It asked adolescents to report on their experience of their friends, and vice versa. Children rated by friends as compassionate and with the ability to share intimate experiences were more likely to feel at ease socially and experienced less depression. Buhrmester argues that, in childhood, friendship centres on play, which includes sharing and co-operation. If children do not develop these skills in middle childhood, the transition to adolescence can become more difficult, and could mean that the adolescent comes to feel isolated at a time when they most need the intimacy of support and understanding from their peers.

Berndt points out that early adolescents are not 'treated as children, but are not treated as adults either' (Berndt, 1982:1447). Consequently children in this age-group are more likely to turn to each other for support. Research by Larson and colleagues (Larson, 2002; Larson et al, 1996), based on self-reports, has shown that early adolescents are more likely to spend time talking to friends than any other single activity, whilst Csikszentmihalyi and colleagues (1977) report that children at this age are most happy when talking to peers. Early adolescents regard close friends as a source of comfort and a place where concerns and feelings can be expressed (Savin-Williams and Berndt, 1990, Azmitia and Lippman, 1999a); children at this age are especially likely to share intimate thoughts and feelings (Berndt, 1981, Douvan and Adelson, 1966) although girls are likely to share more intimate exchanges than boys (Douvan and Adelson, 1966). Mannarino (1978, 1979) found that both male and female adolescents with a best friend whom they regarded as consistently available also reported higher feelings of self esteem than those without such a close friendship. It is interesting to note that changing patterns of friendships at this age (as former friends drift apart, simply do not see each other anymore, or form new and more intense friendships) has been seen as a natural process because of the change of school typically associated with this age-group (Azmitia and Lippman, 1999b) – in some cases it may not be.

The ways children form and maintain friendships at this stage, and the interactions they have with larger groups, are believed to have a significant role in adolescents' psychosocial development (Coleman and Hendry, 1999). Dunn (1996, 2004) in particular has written extensively on the importance of friendship and emotional communication in middle childhood. She describes a teenager who took part in her London research thinking back to the time when she was 10 years old and her parents split up. The fifteen year old recalled that it was at this time her friends became immensely important (2004:70). Friends can additionally act as a buffer between parents and children, especially at times of conflict or trauma.

While attachment theory has been shown to have an influence on the ways in which children can relate to others (Booth-LaForce et al, 2005; Bowlby, 1979), those young people who experience some disruption to their family life may be forced to become 'older' than they really are. This is especially the case if parents are unable to cope with the parental role, either because of family break-up, depression, substance abuse or mental illness. Young people experiencing such confusing and conflicting situations seek help and support - someone who can communicate with them at an emotional level. Booth-LaForce et al. (2005) suggest that friendship can replace inadequate (or lack) of family support and have a direct effect on the psychosocial functioning of children in early adolescence.

The notion of 'popularity' is important to adolescents; the group effect can be both reassuring and allow a sense of experimentation. Coleman and Hendry (1999:150) suggest that 'crowds provide secondary-school pupils with frequent opportunities to experiment with their identity while maintaining a sense of group belonging'. They point out, however, that some children can be unpopular, and that their lack of social encounters may mean that they do not experience the psychosocial exchanges needed to achieve greater social skills.

Peer friendship can also have negative effects on adolescent behaviour. Steinberg and Manahan (2007) found that between the ages of 10 and 14 there were no age differences in resistance to peer influence, resulting in sometimes destructive behavior; however, this resistance rose steadily as adolescents became older, more autonomous, and followed their own values and judgment. It could be argued, therefore, that help and support is needed at an earlier age, before or at the onset of early adolescence.

Cotterell (2007) suggests that schools have important responsibilities with respect to facilitating friendships Their 'fundamental task ... is to create a community where students feel they belong and that their contribution is valued' (2007: 199). Many adolescents prefer to turn to other adolescents rather than other adults (such as school personnel) when seeking support for emotional or traumatic events (Cowie, 1998; Cowie, 1999; Cotterell, 2007). Indeed, Bosacki and Astington (1999) suggest that peers are much more important in early adolescents' *social* lives than teachers, who hardly feature at all. Meanwhile, research by Suldo and Huebner (2006: 198) indicates that 'the effect size associated with support from *classmates* was twice as large as that for support from a close friend', thereby demonstrating the influence of the classroom environment on adolescents' life satisfaction

Friendship may also act as a protective factor against more serious problems. Parry-Langdon (2008) reports that children who had fewer friends at Time 1 were more likely to have persistent conduct disorders at Time 2 three years later. 46% of those who had two to four friends had persistent conduct disorders at Time 2 compared with 35% of those who had five to nine friends. Young people whose parents disapproved of their children's friends or thought that their children's friends were more likely to get into trouble were more likely to have conduct disorders at Time 2 three years later. Also, those who participated less in clubs and groups at school were more likely to have persistent conduct disorders three years on.

The majority of pupils in English schools seem to maintain good relationships with their peers – and draw strength from them. Around 80% of 11 year old boys and girls in the latest HBSC survey covering 2005/06, for example, reported that 'most of the students in (their) classes were kind and helpful' (Currie et al, 2008). The percentages were a little lower amongst 13 and 15 year olds (around two thirds) but again gender differences were small. Nonetheless, a minority of all three age groups did not feel this way. We shall return to some of their problems at a later stage.

Satisfaction with school

Young people's feelings, at least in this age-group, about school seem to be muted and they deteriorate as they get older. The HBSC surveys asked respondents to say how much they 'liked' school (Currie et al, 2008). Just over half of 11 year olds reported that they 'liked school a lot'. However, this response fell away rapidly as they got older – amongst 13 year olds it was less than a third whilst amongst 15 year olds it was as low as a quarter.

Ofsted has initiated a series of TellUs (2007/08) surveys of pupils, asking whether they 'enjoy' school. In 2007, 58% replied that they did either 'always' or 'most of the time'. In 2008, 50% were in these two categories. However, conversely, 50% reported that they only enjoyed school 'sometimes' or 'never' (TellUs3, 2008).

During 2005 Ofsted inspectors rated a variety of school factors in judging schools' effectiveness and amongst these they included a judgement about pupils' 'satisfaction with their school' although it should be noted that this evidence is indirect – inspectors made a judgement on pupils' behalf about how satisfied they were in the school they were inspecting on a seven-point scale (Ofsted, 2005). They report that over 80% were, in their view, 'extremely' or 'highly' satisfied, a figure which, it should be noted, was considerably higher (and perhaps overly optimistic) when compared with the pupils' responses reported earlier. The inspectors also noted a correlation between levels of satisfaction and ethos, attitudes and behaviour: 'where (these) are unsatisfactory, pupils are often dissatisfied with their school, particularly in secondary schools', although they add that whilst there was 'a strong correlation between high attendance and high levels of satisfaction, low attendance (was) not always reflected in low pupil satisfaction' (*op. cit.*: 6).

Whilst caveats about the inspectors' methodology need to be borne in mind some further findings are of interest. In those secondary schools where the 'value-added' contribution to pupils' progress was greatest, pupils were much more likely to be 'extremely/highly' satisfied (*op. cit.*: 12-14). There was also a strong relationship between levels of pupil satisfaction and the 'extent to which the school involved pupils through seeking, valuing and acting on their views' whilst 'good teaching' was also correlated with 'high levels of satisfaction'. They add that 'pupils in secondary schools (were) more intolerant of unsatisfactory or poor teaching' than their primary counterparts.

Using data from the HBSC surveys, research by Samdal et al (1998: 390) provides support for this view. They report that the main predictors of student 'satisfaction' with school were (1) that students feel that they are 'treated fairly'; (2) that they 'feel safe'; and (3) that they perceive their teachers to be 'supportive'. The 'greater the number of these conditions being met, the higher the expected level of satisfaction with school'. They go on to suggest that their research 'has indicated the importance of creating a school environment which the students feel to be safe and justly organized, and which fosters supportive relationships between the students and teachers'. 'Creating such an environment', they argue, 'may have the effect both of improving the educational experience of students and enhancing their wellbeing and health' (Samdal et al, 1998: 394). They suggest that one strategy for achieving this would be to increase the extent to which students feel they are 'participating in decision-making at (their) school'.

Membership of the learning community, participation and voice

Experiencing 'membership' of the learning community and feeling a degree of participation can facilitate young people's sense of engagement. As Rudduck and Flutter (2004: 79) have argued, 'being able to participate is, for pupils, almost synonymous with being engaged …. participation links into issues of ownership and intellectual excitement but it is also about understanding, and thereby having some control over, the nature of the task'.

Croll and colleagues (2008: 397) suggest that, as early as the age of 11, 'children had a strong sense of the instrumental value of school'. However, at the same time, they were also 'making judgements about the extent to which school was committed to them and the relevance of school to them personally'. Their 'general enjoyment of school also included judgements about the extent of bullying and hassle and an appreciation of school as a place for friendships'. Their overall assessments, however, were mediated by the extent to which they envisaged 'doing well'.

Adolescent perceptions are central in this respect. Perceived support enables young people to feel safe and to feel that they belong (Resnick et al 1997; Roeser et al 2000). Young people struggling to explore adult relationships can look to teachers to be more of an objective outsider. They learn about themselves and relationships through relating to teachers and this perceived support is related to self-esteem and depressive feelings. Juvonen (2007) has emphasised the relationship between perceived support and educational risk as others have emphasised the link to emotional risk (Roeser et al 1998). Johnson (2008) and Juvonen (2007) also single out the importance of perceived fairness in these relationships, which in turn links to the development of trust (Csikszentmihalyi & Nakamura, 1998; Deci, 1992) and more generally to achievement (Wentzel 1998). In the same vein, Voelkl (200: 136) reports for a large sample of US students that those 'in schools with perceived positive atmospheres may be more encouraged, like school better, and become engaged; this increased engagement may, in turn, stimulate them to work harder, thus fostering higher achievement. Without the mediating effect of student participation, however, a warm atmosphere may have little or no impact on fostering higher achievement'

Other key elements are related to autonomy and agency. Research studies show that students value highly engagement in decision making and processes within a relationship that allow for some autonomy. Schools that were strong on personalized learning, for example, tended to be characterized by a high degree of pupil engagement and participation (Sebba et al, 2007). Johnson (2008) also emphasises the agency of the teacher (i.e. the teacher intervening on behalf of or in the best interests of the pupils' wellbeing, arguing that conceptions of teachers are strongly action oriented, and that children have high expectations of teachers' levels of efficacy and power to influence. Gorard and Smith (2008) have also shown that that students' reported treatment at the hands of other students and teachers in their school was an important predictor of whether they adopted values such as 'tolerance of others'.

A key feature here is that what really matters is what students *feel* is the reality. A study of 10-15 year olds in the USA by Skinner et al (2008) found that adolescents' perceptions of teacher support moderately predicted their engaged behaviour across the school year but teachers' own perceptions of how much support they gave their pupils did not have any effect. They concluded that it is adolescents' *perceptions* of support that influence behavioural outcomes rather than the extent of the support which they are actually given. The study also reinforced the finding reported in the previous paragraph that adolescents' perceptions of autonomy in learning were moderate predictors of engaged learning behavior.

How far young people in England feel actively engaged in the life of their school is more difficult to establish. An HBSC survey showed that, along with variables discussed earlier, 'participation in setting (school) rules' was correlated with 'life satisfaction' although again not particularly strongly (Currie et al, 2000). We also think there may have been some modest improvement in recent years as schools have become more familiar with the ideas of student 'voice'. Nonetheless, in the most recent Ofsted survey, 34% of those questioned said their views were 'not listened to in the running of their school' (TellUs3, 2008).

Pressure of schoolwork

As children get older they are frequently exposed to more formal assessments of their academic performance. In the English system this pressure is potentially exacerbated by the prevalence of national systems of testing whose results are subsequently made public through performance tables. As Layard, Dunn and colleagues (2009: 103-4) have suggested, 'testing and league tables are becoming central to the motivation system of children and teachers' and 'cast a cloud', both 'emotional' and 'intellectual', with too little room 'for teaching related to feelings or social commitment'. Harlen and Crick (2002) have also pointed out that English pupils have become some of the most tested in the world. One side-effect of these efforts to expose teachers to greater scrutiny has been that young people have become more aware of the need to achieve as well as the various pressures that can flow from it.

It is difficult to be precise about the effects of increased testing on young people's sense of wellbeing and the direct evidence is very limited. Davies and Brember (1998) report that, with the introduction of testing into primary schools, low-attaining children had significantly lower self-esteem than previously. However, the age-group was significantly younger than the group with which we are mainly concerned and there is some reason to question the causal direction.

The HBSC surveys have asked young people about the extent to which they felt 'pressured' by their schoolwork (Currie et al, 2008) and their responses are reproduced in Table 3 below. Amongst 11 year olds roughly four out of ten reported that they felt 'some' or 'a lot' of pressure from schoolwork. This rose to around half amongst 13 year olds whilst the figures for England amongst 15 year olds were higher still. Some 60% of boys in this age-group felt 'pressured' along with some 70% of girls. Feelings of being 'pressured' increased amongst their counterparts in other countries as well; the average for the HBSC samples rose from around a quarter of 11 year olds to just under half 15 year olds. But, interestingly, the responses of this older age-group were not that different to those of the younger age-group in England.

Figures from a recent Ofsted survey (TellUs2, 2007) provide similar estimates; again perceptions of pressure rose considerably amongst the older age group whilst a national survey of secondary school pupils reported that around four in ten felt fewer exams would make school more enjoyable (MORI, 2004). The estimates from the research commissioned by *The Good Childhood Inquiry* also generated comparable data (Pople, 2009). Just under half the participants (47%) agreed with the statement that they 'worried about their schoolwork' and over half (58%) said they were worried about their exams.

Table 3: Pupils' perceptions of feeling pressured by schoolwork

11 Year Olds	2005/2006 Feeling 'some' or 'lot of' pressure (%)
English Boys	43
English Girls	37
HBSC Boys	24
HBSC Girls	27
13 Year Olds	
English Boys	48
English Girls	48
HBSC Boys	35
HBSC Girls	38
15 Year Olds	
English Boys	60
English Girls	70
HBSC Boys	40
HBSC Girls	49

Source: HBSC Survey, Currie et al (2008)

Another question asked in the HBSC surveys reinforces the view that exam stress and perceptions of declining performance increase with age. Young people were asked to judge how, in their opinion, their 'class teacher(s) thought about their school performance compared to their classmates' (Currie et al, 2008). Their responses are given in Table 4. Younger pupils were considerably more optimistic.

Table 4: Pupils' perceptions of their own school performance

	2005/2006 Performance perceived as 'good' or 'very good' (%)
11 Year Olds	
English Boys	76
English Girls	80
HBSC Boys	70
HBSC Girls	77
13 Year Olds	
English Boys	68
English Girls	75
HBSC Boys	60
HBSC Girls	66
15 Year Olds	
English Boys	66
English Girls	67
HBSC Boys	53
HBSC Girls	59

Source: HBSC Survey, Currie et al (2008)

The idea of 'school connectedness' brings together a number of potentially disparate elements in the literature. When an institution takes them seriously it can enhance their effects; although no single element is overwhelmingly important their combination is potentially quite powerful. The prognosis in terms of social and emotional wellbeing is good for young people who relate well to their teachers, find their peers supportive, are broadly satisfied with what their school is doing for them; see themselves as part of a learning community which listens to them; and are able to handle the pressures.

Thinking 'Small'

A number of studies have sought to link the attitudinal dimensions of schooling to structural and organisational components although those which have considered pupils' attitudes are rather limited by comparison with those on aspects of academic achievement. In a systematic review of the research on school size, Garrett et al (2004) concluded that there was a negative relationship between school size and children's (and their teachers') perceptions. McNeely et al (2002) found that pupils in larger US schools reported less school connectedness whilst Silins and Mulford (2000) found lower levels of student participation in Australian high schools.

In practice, the range of school sizes in the UK is fairly restricted by comparison with those prevailing in some other societies. Only 2%, for example, of secondary schools have more than 1800 pupils whilst only 1% have fewer than 300. More than 50% of English secondary schools have between 700 and 1200 pupils. Nonetheless, such research as there is does suggest that children's attitudes decline with size although the findings on maladaptive behaviours are more inconsistent (Newman, 2008). Lee and Burham (2003) report that students were a little less likely to drop out of small schools compared with those in medium and large ones.

Of course, there is no necessary reason why large schools should have less favourable outcomes than smaller ones – school organisation can take multiple forms. There has been some experimentation, especially in the USA, to make schools seem 'smaller' by such devices as creating 'schools within schools', house systems and pastoral care structures. Unfortunately, research evidence on the outcomes of these developments in terms of wellbeing outcomes is in short supply.

The work of Thompson and colleagues (2006) is one of the few exceptions. Combining data from the HBSC surveys with national databases and a tailored school survey, their research covered a sample of over 300 US schools serving grades 6-10. They reported lower levels of school connectedness in larger schools. It should be noted, however, that the effect was very small and, bearing in mind the range of proposals the authors made for improving connectedness, not seen as particularly important.

Kahne and colleagues (2008) have recently explored some of the implications of the 'small' high school reforms in Chicago. This is an especially interesting development because it tracks what might happen in other systems if they moved over to small-school structures. They concluded that 'small schools appear to prompt a pathway to personalised support and improved attendance and, perhaps, graduation' (2008: 296). They had hypothesised that a 'supportive student context' would influence future expectations, both amongst students and teachers, lead to more respectful classroom behaviour, increase peer support for achievement and sense of belonging, boost classroom 'personalisation' and build stronger networks of student-teacher trust and teacher support. However, whilst effects were noted, most of them were fairly modest and dropped off a little in the second year of the reform's initiation. The researchers were less convinced about the impact of the reforms on other aspects of the high schools' functioning. 'We saw evidence that smaller schools enable the creation of contexts for teachers (ones characterised by greater trust, commitment and sense of influence) but that these contexts do not appear to be fostering more systematic efforts at instructional improvement, different instructional practices and improved performance on standardised tests' (2008: 299). 'If the key lies in supportive and personalised settings, then small schools need not be the only way that this goal is achieved'.

Another American research project (Felner et al, 2001) has explored the impact of smaller learning communities as a way of dealing with declining attitudes at school transfer. This team intervened on a number of occasions over two decades to establish cohorts of no more than 150 pupils which had a small team of teachers for all subjects and a dedicated team of teachers looking after them in their post-transfer year. Being involved in the STEP initiative, they report, was related to a 40-50% reduction in school dropout rates and somewhat lower levels of social, emotional, behavioural problems and difficulties with substance abuse.

There has been a similar initiative in the UK supported by Human Scale Education. Some fifty large secondary schools were encouraged to develop 'human scale principles and practices' (Tasker, 2008). This initiative seems to have persuaded government to experiment to a limited extent with small school remodelling. However, more recently, despite funding an initiative at Bishops Park, a large comprehensive school (Fielding et al, 2006), the DCSF has decided that its position on school size is 'neutral' (DCSF, 2008).

Much of the discussion about wellbeing outcomes has been conducted at the level of the school. In an interesting departure Torsheim and Wold (2001) explored variations in 'health complaints' between different classes within the same schools. Using data from the Norwegian component of the HBSC surveys and a multi-level statistical model, they noted that most of the variation in outcomes was between individuals. They did not test simultaneously for school and class level variation but, at the institutional level, a sizeable component of the variation between students in health complaints was associated with membership of different classes. Some were reported by their members to be 'noisier' than others and this, in turn, was connected to higher reports of health complaints. The extent to which members of the same classes made similar observations strengthened the researchers' view that this was a real effect.

A national study conducted by Blatchford et al (2008) considered the links between class size and various achievement–related and attitudinal outcomes. They report that in smaller classes pupils interacted more with teachers and that pupils' classroom engagement increased. Class size seemed to have a disproportional impact on low-attaining pupils whose classroom engagement declined in larger classes whilst teachers spent more time attempting to control them.

There are nonetheless some surprising gaps and omissions in this area of research. As one of a number of strategies for developing 'smaller' structures which relate more closely to students, most schools adopt forms of pastoral organisation such as year groups, house groups or form tutor systems. Marland (2002), a central figure in the development of pastoral systems from the 1970s onwards, comments that the challenge in large schools is to find ways of ensuring that 'careful supervision of progress of the individual is the responsibility of someone who has under his care a manageable number of pupils'.

Whilst such approaches are well-established, however, and are clearly intended to foster greater levels of student support, we were able to identify hardly any recent research which linked these structures to improved wellbeing outcomes, a small-scale study by Schofield (2007) being the sole exception. Nor could we find any systematic empirical evidence on the impact of tutor groups although a special issue of *Pastoral Care in Education* (20, 4) was devoted to this question.

The organisation of subject teaching and one-to-one teaching as well as combinations of teaching approaches may also affect wellbeing outcomes. Whilst a number of studies have explored students' preferences for different teaching approaches, again none in recent times appear to have directly considered their implications for wellbeing. There has been a small amount of work on groupwork however. Pell et al (2007) found that positive attitudes towards groupwork were related to positive attitudes towards school whilst Dolmans and Schmidt (2007) concluded that small group tutorials could stimulate intrinsic interest in a subject.

The effects of new school buildings on pupils' attitudes have received scant attention until recently. A study some two decades ago pointed out that the built environment could cause stress (Conners, 1983). Rudd et al (2008) recently surveyed pupils before and after the re-opening of a new school. Pupils reported increased pride in the school and said that they felt safer in the new school environment. There was also a small increase in those reporting that they 'enjoyed' school.

There is one further structural element of schooling on which we need to comment. Schools in most educational systems are designed to cater for specific age-ranges of pupils (5-11, 11-16, 5-8, 10-14, 14-18 and so on depending on the type of organisation that has been adopted). Whenever these organisational breaks occur, pupils must transfer from one school to another. We review the evidence on transfer in the next chapter. Suffice it to say here that the research on transfer is generally consistent with the studies we have reviewed in the previous pages on the 'supportive school'. Transfer research also indicates that young people have deteriorating perceptions of teachers in secondary school, experience declining attitudes to school, increase their reliance on peers, and sometimes experience difficulties as old friendships fade and new ones emerge.

Social climate or academic focus?

The central thrust in recent years of much government policy for raising educational standards, both in the UK and elsewhere, has concentrated on the academic focus of schools' activities. Much less attention has been paid to matters which might directly affect pupil wellbeing such as a school's social climate. Indeed, the greater majority of studies have focused either on academic results or, more rarely, on social outcomes. Consequently, it has been difficult to clarify whether the pursuit of one outcome is necessarily at the expense of the other.

An evaluation of Comer's School Development Program by Cook and colleagues (1999: 544) provides some of the only evidence available. The main reason for this is that, as Cook puts it, 'James Comer contends that a wide range of student skills can be enhanced ....by improving the interpersonal relationships and social climate in a school as a prelude to enhancing its academic focus'. Cook and colleagues (1999: 577) report that in the 23 US middle schools they studied the correlation between a school's social climate and its academic focus was just below 0.4; a school's social climate was also correlated with a school's SES although rather weakly (correlation of 0.2). A series of analyses designed to probe the interactions between social climate and academic focus, however, led Cook and colleagues to conclude that there was no evidence that 'combining a better social and academic climate qualitatively transforms a school'. 'The fairest conclusion', they comment, is that 'a school's social climate promotes psychological and social well-being but not academic achievement which it might even lower' (*op. cit:* 579).

This broad conclusion is reinforced by some Dutch evidence. Knuver and Brandsma (1993: 201) studied two age-groups (9/10 and 11/12) in the later stages of primary school. They report school-level correlations between pupils' achievement in language and arithmetic and a measure of 'school wellbeing' as 0.17 and 0.04. By any standards, they conclude, these correlations are not sufficiently high that one could assert that 'schools which are effective in the cognitive domain are also effective with respect to affective outcomes on the whole one can interpret the two domains as relatively independent'.

Conclusions

There are a number of dimensions to the 'supportive school'. Such institutions seem to pay attention to young people's relationships with their teachers, with each other, to their general satisfaction with their educational experiences and to their feelings about their membership of the school as a learning community in which they actively participate. They also seem to be aware of the detrimental effects the pressures of academic work, testing and examinations can exert on their charges and seek to find ways of helping them to deal with the consequences. They may well adopt some elements of 'thinking small' strategies in their organisation and culture in relation to pastoral and wellbeing issues. In the process 'supportive schools' attempt to enhance their students' sense of 'connectedness', both with the institution and the learning experience.

Whilst we have been able to use the literature to specify the various dimensions of the 'supportive school' there are, nonetheless, considerable gaps in the research. Few researchers have taken a holistic view; consequently we have not been able to establish how the different parts relate to each other. The US evaluation by Cook and colleagues (1999) strongly suggests that schools will need to develop policies for their pupils' academic achievement and separate policies for their psychological wellbeing - there may be some overlap but not enough to assume that policies in one area will necessarily have effects in the other. And, crucially, we have not been able to establish how prevalent such 'supportive' institutions might be across the English school system.

CHAPTER FIVE

FROM PRIMARY TO SECONDARY

Two perspectives have tended to dominate the debate about transfer and these are reflected in the way that many Local Authorities and schools tackle the issue. The first of these might be described as a theory *of gradual change* whereby it is argued that transfer works best when the school environment matches the gradual changes taking place in the psychological needs and dispositions of the young adolescent. In the United States this *stage–environment-fit* hypothesis was first proposed by Eccles *et al* (1989; Eccles, Midgley, & Adler, 1984) and was based on the person–environment fit theories of Mitchell (1969) and Hunt (1975).

According to Eccles and her colleagues, dips in both pupils' attitudes and attainment are a consequence of a poor fit between the young adolescents' developmental stage and the school environment. In particular, the growing desire of young adults to make their own decisions about where to go, what to do and whom to do it with, together with 'goal aspirations' or the stirrings within an individual of what s/he would like to do on reaching adulthood, are often in sharp contrast with the situation as it exists after transfer from primary or elementary school, where pupils experience more competition, less freedom to make their own decisions and work that consists mainly of teacher-dominated classroom discourse with learning tightly controlled by the teacher. Other research in the United States (Miller, 1986) suggests that the onset of puberty tends to coincide with an improved capacity in pupils to identify any dissonance that may exist between their *ideal* school environment and the *actual* reality. Hence transfer around the ages 11 to 13 is particularly thought to be a crucial stage in pupils' development.

Although not expressed in terms of the above ideas, person-environment matching was used in the United Kingdom in the 1970s to support the argument for a three-tier arrangement in which middle schools provided a bridge between the primary and secondary ethoses for learning (Hargreaves & Tickle, 1980). Some Local Authorities found the concept of a middle school very attractive because it enabled them to convert to comprehensive education using existing school buildings and without increasing capacity. Thus it was argued that there was a key period in the life of pupils as they moved from childhood to adolescence requiring a special kind of school (Schools Council, 1972), supported by findings from the Plowden Report (CACE, 1967). However, whether this period took place from the ages of 8-12 or 9-13 often seemed to depend on the number and size of the available schools buildings in the particular Local Authority. The 'stage-environment fit' therefore attempts to build on what has gone before in helping pupils to become 'autonomous learners' (Gorwood, 1986). In practice, Galton and Willcocks (1983) found that whether the middle school covered the 8-12, 9-13 or 10-14 range, Year 7 was marked by a high degree of discontinuity and, since the introduction of the National Curriculum in the late 1980s, the shift from Key Stage 2 to Key Stage 3 at this age has served to reinforce this trend.

An alternative view offers a different perspective on the transfer process. Borrowing from anthropology, it makes use of the concept of 'status passage' (Measor & Woods, 1984). In most societies the move from childhood to adolescence, or indeed any change in status, involves a number of special rites which are designed to initiate an individual into their new role(s). Accompanying this change in status there is likely to be a degree of folklore which includes myths about what happens during the induction process. Transfer, when viewed in this light, bears many of the hallmarks of a status passage. Going to the 'big school' marks a point in time when 'grown ups', such as parents and teachers, no longer see pupils as children but as young adults. Initiation into the big school involves a series of rituals to do with new subjects, moving to teachers in different parts of the building rather than spending time in a single classroom and learning how to cope with different organisational arrangements, such as mastering the procedure for selecting one's lunch from a cafeteria style self-service menu. Accompanying this change in status are certain myths such as "*the royal flush*" whereby new pupils are alleged to have their heads held down the lavatory bowl while another pupil pulls the chain. Such myths appear to be global.

Measor and Woods (1984) point out that the view of the transfer process as a status passage is at odds with the previous notion that the main tasks of the primary and secondary school are to ensure that there is as much continuity as possible. These authors argue that if the process of transfer was so managed that the changes before and after the move to the big school were minimised, then pupils would have little evidence to suggest a change in status. The desire for continuity needs to be balanced by an element of discontinuity which recognises the need in pupils for some 'outward signs' that they are successfully managing the change from childhood to young adolescence. The apprehension, mingled with excitement, which arises during the transfer process is therefore largely a result of this continuity-discontinuity mix. This can be seen in the way that pupils talk about their hopes and fears during the last few weeks of primary school. They worry about losing existing friends but are looking forward to making new ones. They are looking forward to doing new subjects but worry whether they can cope with the work. In the same way they are favourably disposed towards having more teachers but are concerned about whether some teachers will be too strict. In this version of events transfer is full of these kinds of dilemmas. Some secondary schools take the status passage approach to the extreme in that the contrasts with the primary world are sharply defined from day one of the new term. Pupils are tested and then streamed or placed in bands for key subjects (languages, mathematics and science), they move rooms between classes and share the same playground and dinner queues. Few schools would appear to regularly review this continuity-discontinuity balance to take into account changing trends in primary and secondary education. In contrast to the stage–environment theory, where changes are managed over time to match the pupils' biological and physiological development, the 'status passage' approach, in its extreme form, is marked by instant and total immersion into the transfer school environment.

In practice, during the 1970/80 period, the view that saw primary schools as places of exciting innovations and secondary schools as dull, formal and hidebound by tradition, was often based on rhetoric. Galton *et al.* (1980) demonstrated that most primary classes were not hubs of creativity in reality in which children discovered things for themselves, nor did pupils work for a large part of the time cooperatively in groups and nor were these places where pupils participated in the decision making. Other studies, notably those of Mortimore *et al.* (1988) and Alexander *et al.* (1989) confirmed that this was indeed the case so that although classroom organisation differed between the primary and secondary school (groups versus single/pair seating) the forms of instruction were very similar. More recently, Webb and Vulliamy (2006) found that 18 out of the 45 primary classrooms visited now had desks or tables arranged in rows and as did other observational studies (Alexander, 2000; Hargreaves & Galton, 2002). Indeed, Smith *et al* . (2004) suggest there has been a reversal in trends in primary schools whereby the teaching, like that in the first year of the secondary school, is mainly interrogative and directive in nature. Viewing the process of transfer as a status passage would suggest that one of the reasons for the persistent decline in attitudes comes about because pupils expect to be taught in different ways after transfer.

However, this rarely turns out to be the case, particularly in the core subjects of mathematics and science where, as will be shown later in the review, the dips in attitude are steepest.

Pre- and Post-transfer Perceptions

For the majority of pupils the immediate anxieties (or more usually apprehension mixed with anticipation) associated with transfer appear relatively short lived, There is remarkable agreement on this point when studies spanning four decades are compared. Youngman (1978) and Youngman and Lunzer (1977) found only 20 % of pupils in England retained negative feelings after one term in the transfer school, a conclusion supported by Spelman (1979) in Northern Ireland and by Dutch and McCall (1974) in Scotland. More recently, Evangelou *et al* . (2008) have reported that 75% of pupils said they had adjusted well by the end of their first term in the transfer school. Among the pupils who failed to adjust within a short period, between 6%-10% have reported persistent problems (ILEA, 1986; Chedzoy & Burden, 2005b). Galton and Willocks (1983) found that for only about 12% of pupils were the dips in attainment sustained and relatively serious. Not surprisingly, a majority of pupils who have difficulty adjusting at transfer tend to have special educational needs (Muldoon, 2005). Evangelou *et al.* (2008) reported that some 12% of SEN pupils had experienced bullying in their first term although the same authors claim that in general SEN pupils reported that they had adjusted quickly and successfully to their new school. These results are based on surveys of pupil opinion. Those who favour more qualitative approaches (e.g. Rudduck, Chaplain, & Wallace, 1996) argue that the negative effects of transition are more prolonged, particularly in relation to friendships, work and relating to teachers.

Any differences here are partly to do with semantics in that these latter concerns are regarded by many writers as ongoing problems of adolescence and schooling of which transfer is but an extreme case. Most of these concerns can be classified under six distinct headings:

1. Personal adaptability: Concerns about being the youngest and smallest and about fitting in with older pupils
2. Peers: Making new friends, keeping old ones, and bullying
3. Teachers: Adjusting to several teachers and of increasing teacher strictness
4.   Size: Getting lost, not using the authorized routes, etc.

5. Work: Coping with different subjects and doing homework on time
6. Moving: Getting to school on time, learning the rules, bringing the right books and equipment, buying school dinners, getting a locker.

To explore these issues further, and in particular in relation to their implications for wellbeing, twenty four studies that gathered data on adolescents' perceptions surrounding school transition were identified for the literature review. From these, 12 studies which had both pre- and post-transition data were selected for use in a meta-analysis to ensure longitudinal validity. The most common negative and positive perceptions (pre- and post-transfer) cited by children in each study were coded and tallied within codes to compile the charts. These studies span the years 1980 to 2008 and come from the UK, Finland, the USA, Australia and New Zealand (see Appendix 2 for details). The six categories were formed inductively to cover the types of perceptions that were most commonly mentioned. There were no outliers in the data.

The results of these various studies are displayed in Figure 6 which shows the number of studies (n) which revealed negative (left hand side of Figure 6) and positive perceptions (right hand side of same figure). The studies were also separated into those which related to pre-transfer perceptions and post-transfer perceptions.

What issues emerged most frequently? The positive perceptions surrounding transfer were about having coped well with the move (n=7) despite previous anxieties. Many pupils are successful in keeping and making new friends (n=6) and in finding their way around school (n=2). Some adolescents report liking the change of teachers (n=3) and the extra provision of resources for drama and sport (n=3). However, the greater bulk of perceptions appear to take the form of worries. The most frequent concerns expressed before transfer deal with making new friends and retaining old ones from the primary school, and being bullied by older pupils (n=9). The second most commonly expressed concern is about harder work and coping with homework (n=7). Pupils also worry about getting used to school buildings and being lost (n=6).

Figure 6: Pre- and Post-Transfer Perceptions

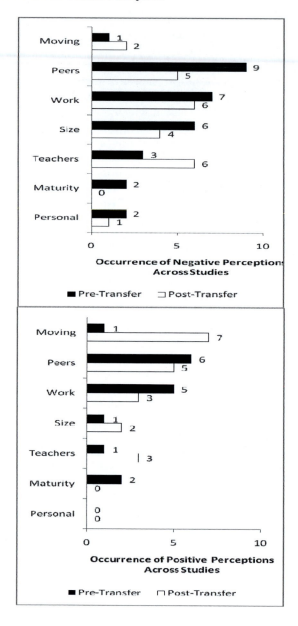

Following transfer several of these issues are realised. On work related issues (n=6) the emphasis tends to have shifted (see Figure 6). There are fewer concerns about coping and more expressions of disappointment about the repetitive nature of the curriculum activities (Spelman 1979; Brown & Armstrong 1982; Suffolk LEA 1999; Hargreaves & Galton 2002). Some pupils have problems finding their way around the new school initially (n=4) although reports show that this soon abates. Worries about peers decrease but there are still some difficulties with bullying and with making friends in the new school (n=5). Interestingly, a problem anticipated by few has become the blight of many – teachers in the post-transfer schools are stricter and present a challenge to adjustment with their multiple teaching styles and expectations (n=6). There are worries about the ways that teachers apply school rules, including the tendency of some teachers to punish the whole class for an individual's misdemeanour (Brown & Armstrong 1982; Suffolk LEA 2001; Caulfield *et al.*2005). Concerns about teachers and about the nature of the work appear to be a major determinant of changes in pupils' attitudes over the transfer period.

Meta-Analysis of Psychological Measures

A second analysis attempted to define whether similarities existed in changes in pupils' psychology across transfer in different contexts and through time. A total of 17 studies (4 from the UK, 12 from the USA and 1 from Canada) yielded data on various psychological and attitudinal measures over the pre- and post-transfer year, thus allowing trends in excess of a twelve month period to be examined (see Appendix 2 for details). Each study used the same measuring instruments on each occasion and provided means and standard deviations so that effect sizes could be calculated using Cohen's (1988) criterion. The various measures were usually administered towards the end of the last term in the feeder (pre-transfer) school, during the first term after transfer and then again at some point during the remainder of the year. Various issues encountered in handling these studies are also discussed in Appendix 2.

Changes in Attitude to School and to Subjects
across Transfer

Figures 7, 8a, 8b and 8c present estimates of the changes in attitude to school and to subjects. Both these sets of studies along with others which did not fit the selection criteria for the meta-analysis reveal similar patterns in changing attitudes. Consequently their findings are discussed jointly throughout this section. They show that overall attitudes to school decline in most of the developed countries (Haladyna & Thomas, 1979; Simon & Ward, 1982; Hirsch & Rapkin, 1987; Galton, Comber, & Pell, 2002; Greenhough et al., 2007). They also indicate that the sharpest decline generally takes place after the first term in the transfer school (Cotterell, 1986; Berndt & Mekos, 1995; Benner & Graham, 2007). Although Dutch & McCall (1974) and Hirsch & Rapkin (1986) found that more able pupils had better attitudes, more recent studies (Galton *et al.* 2003) and Pell *et al* .(2007) have found negative correlations between enjoyment of school and teachers' estimates of pupils' ability.

Figure 7: Attitudes to School

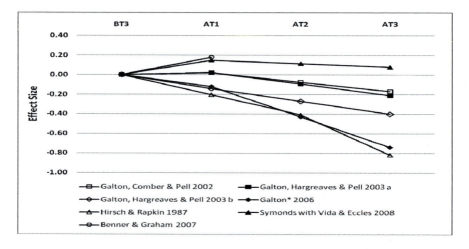

Figures 8a, 8b and 8c show changes in attitudes towards individual subjects (English, mathematics and science). Nearly all the studies show a decline over the transfer period but the trajectories differ. In the UK, English tends to maintain or improve its pre-transfer level but declines thereafter (BEDC 1975; Galton *et al.* 2003), whilst it shows a slight improvement across time in the USA (Eccles *et al.* 1989). In mathematics the decline is continuous (Eccles *et al.* 1989; Galton *et al.* 2003). Science tends to show the sharpest deviations, especially for girls (Hargreaves & Galton, 2002; Galton et al., 2003). There is a difficulty, however, in distinguishing between a general year-by-year decline in attitudes to school and to subjects, both in the primary and the lower secondary school, and any declines that are due specifically to any 'transfer effect'.

Figure 8a: Attitudes to English

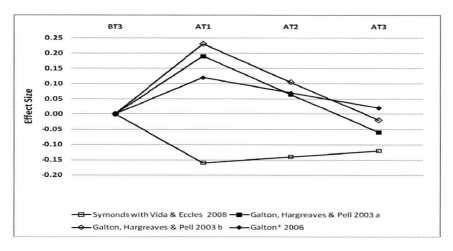

8b. Attitudes to Maths

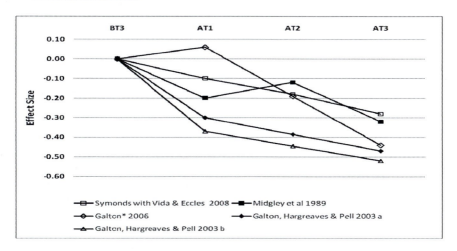

8c. Attitudes to Science

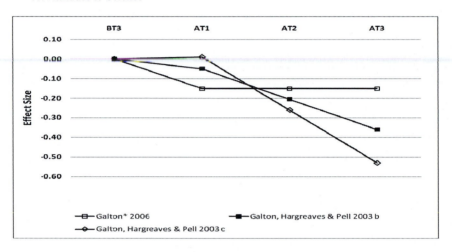

Many studies have noted a gender difference in declining attitudes to science across transfer, with girls having lower scores (Brown, 1976; Doherty & Dawe, 1985; Francis & Greer, 1999). Barmby *et al* . (2008) found that the largest dips in attitude between Year 7 and Year 9 concerned *learning science in school.* The decline was greatest between Years 7 and 8 and Years 9 and 10. These dips in attitudes towards science at secondary level appear to be a consistent trend spanning several decades and predating the more recent decline at primary level reported by Osborne *et al.* (2003) and by Tymms *et al.* (2008). Other studies, mostly from the USA, have produced similar results (Simpson & Oliver, 1985; Yager & Yager, 1985; George 2000; George 2006) although the gender contrasts are not so marked. In Australia, Baird *et al* .(1990) found dips in science attitude at transfer as did Speering and Rennie (1996) where the decline was sharper for girls. These dips appeared to continue in subsequent years.

Dips in attitudes to science and a continued decline in scores as pupils move through the lower secondary school therefore appear to be a characteristic of most developed countries around the world but there are indications that the trend may be more marked in the UK. This position is supported by international comparisons such as The Trends in International Mathematics and Science Study (TIMMS). In the latest TIMSS administration, England was in bottom place among 36 countries in terms of the rating '*liking science*' (Martin, Mullis & Foy, 2008).

There is some evidence to suggest that the rate of decline in attitudes is dependent on the age of transfer and school organisation. Spelman (1979) found transfer to the middle school of a three-tier system resulted in smaller dips than when eventually pupils moved on to the secondary school while Jennings and Hargreaves (1981) reported that pupils who transferred to a middle school on the same site were more positive about school than were their peers who moved to an off-site secondary school.

Change in Self-Oriented Psychology across School Transfer

Psychological measures employed in transfer studies have included academic self-concept, social adaptation, various measures of achievement motivation, self-esteem and school-based anxiety. In all, seventeen studies were identified for this part of the analysis (see Appendix 2 for further details).

Figure 9 plots the mean value of the effect sizes for the studies which considered academic self-concept. There were no clear trends however; some studies suggested it declined but others indicated trends in the opposite direction. This may suggest that both schools and cohort differences have a role in determining whether an adolescent will feel good about themselves as a learner, and about their achievement, after they change schools. The divergence of trajectories for both samples in Youngman and Lunzer's study (1977) show that particular measures of academic self-concept cannot be held entirely responsible for the observed differences.

Figure 9: Academic Self-Concept Across Transfer

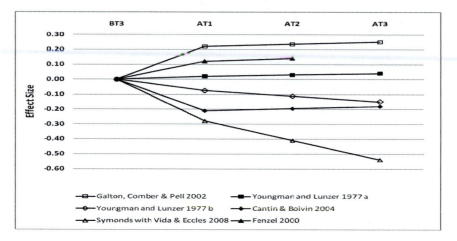

Figure 10 plots the mean effect sizes for the five other areas considered under the general heading of psychological disposition. The very limited number of studies available for analysis here resulted in a decision to only group together those studies which had the same direction of effect.

Figure 10: Trends in Psychological Disposition Across Transfer

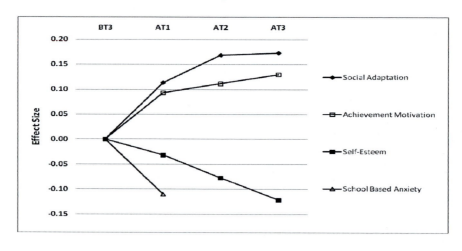

Looking at the trends in the figure above, we can see a positive effect on social adaptation and achievement motivation over the transfer period. Self-esteem is the only measure (other than attitudes to school as discussed previously) which appears to have a negative psychological change. The observed decline in school related anxiety is, of course, a positive occurrence, showing that adolescents moving between schools are soon relieved of nervous feelings in relation to their new school environment.

When examining each of these areas in more detail, it seems that several factors are at play in the construction of the trends. For social adaptation, this involves (as previously stated) positive reflections on making a new and better matched group of friends. Specific measurements of peer support included: friendship quality (Wargo-Aikins et al. 2005); close friend support and social competence (Fenzel 2000); social efficacy expectations (Siedman 1994); social acceptance (Cantin & Boivin 2004); and peer relations (Crockett et al. 1989). These were all found to increase as adolescents move between schools. Similarly, feelings of isolation and loneliness (Galton et al. 2002, 2003), hassles with peers (Siedman 1994) and peer-strain (Fenzel 2000) were found to decrease. The latter measures were reversed in the analysis. As reported in a qualitative study of perceptions (Pratt & George 2005), adolescents' need for supportive friendships increases over the transfer period as, one can surmise, friends aid each other in coping – especially if they experience the move together. However, Blyth et al. (1978) found that adolescents' preference for friends' company over parents' rose across Grades 6 to 7 in both transfer (elementary to junior high school) and non-transfer (K-8) samples. Taken with the above information, and in light of suggestions about adolescent behaviour (Eccles & Midgley 1989), this indicates that increasing peer-orientation may be common during early adolescence in general and that it can be exacerbated by the process of school transfer.

Another change across transfer that may relate to adolescent development is the increase in motivation to do well and achieve at school, as documented by many studies, despite the same adolescents having declining attitudes to school at this time. Motivation can be seen as *intrinsic* to the act of learning, where satisfaction is gained from within the studying itself, or as *extrinsic*, which is a response to certain external demands such as learning for a specific purpose, as in gaining a necessary qualification in pursuit of a certain career path. *Achievement* motivation represents a drive for success by reaching a certain goal (Brophy, 1999) and generally appears to increase or to remain stable across transfer (Seidman *et al.*1994; Galton *et al.*2003) although Seifert and Schulz

(2007) in their analysis of the National Longitudinal Survey of Children and Youth have noted a decline in the move from elementary school.

Pupils with a strong sense of their own competence will believe that hard work and extra effort will allow them to succeed. Students who feel that they can achieve through their own efforts will be displaying high levels of *mastery* motivation (Dweck, 1986). These students will not be concerned about their progress in relation to others. Anxious students are particularly 'at risk' from fear of failure in a competitive culture (Covington, 1992). The current emphasis on performance in schools (in the form of target setting, Standard Assessment Tasks and school performance 'league tables') is likely to inhibit the growth of mastery motivation and discourage intrinsic motivation.

Pell *et al.* (2007) have investigated the nature of motivation in the present day English classrooms of the lower secondary school. These researchers found that achievement motivation was now less concerned with competition (getting top marks) and more to do with the satisfaction of gaining the appropriate level on National Tests. Academic satisfaction as a form of achievement motivation remained high and stable throughout the lower secondary school. A more important change has occurred with regard to achievement mastery where the focus has shifted away from the intrinsic drive. Whether or not the pupil finds the subject matter interesting now appears to have little or no effect on progress or achieving the necessary goals. Studies that did not meet specific criteria for the above analysis include Zanobini and Usai (2002) who found that general intrinsic motivation decreases across transfer, and study by Muldoon (2005) where decreases in 'learning goal orientation', which also reflects intrinsic interest in the subject, were found. In keeping with the attitude surveys the decline in intrinsic motivation is greater in some subjects such as mathematics (Rogers et al., 1994).

As only one study found had usable data for general self-concept, no mean effect size was calculated for this domain. However, based on the findings of this study and on other literature, we can infer that general self-concepts tended to increase or remain stable over the transfer period for both genders (Simon & Ward, 1982; Chung *et al.*1998; Gillison, Standage, & Skevington, 2008). Part of the increase can be attributed to general all-round development. In relation to this, delaying transfer and remaining within a more supportive primary or elementary school environment appears to result in higher levels of self-concept (Eccles et al., 1991). Support for this finding comes from a transfer study by the Inner London Education Authority (ILEA 1986) who found that whereas 3.8% of explained variance in self-concept could be attributed to the pupils' background, gender and age, 8.4% was a consequence of school differences.

Despite increases in global self-concept (e.g. 'I am the type of person who does well at school, sport and in my friendships'), measures of self-oriented self-esteem (e.g. 'I feel good about myself every day'), personal image, body image and self-confidence reveal declining perceptions at transition. They clearly indicate that girls are more affected at transfer than boys (Blyth et al., 1978; Galton *et al.* 2002; Cantin & Boivin, 2004). Subsequent reanalysis of Blyth's data by Simmons *et al.*(1979) suggested that the onset of puberty in girls accentuated this decline and a similar finding emerged from Petersen and Crockett's (1985) study that used pupils' perceptions of 'body image' as an indicator of self image. Eccles *et al.* (1989) also found that the decline in self esteem was greatest immediately after transfer and was strongly associated with other psychological and social problems. There is also evidence that multiple transitions accelerate the decline in self-esteem (Jones & Thornburg, 1985) . Such transitions included other changes apart from moving schools such as moving home, entering puberty and changing relationships. West *et al* (2008) whose measures were administered two, four and six years after transfer, found that at around 15 years concerns about peer relationships at transfer were the best predictor of self-esteem whereas at 18 years it was concerns about the school and work which were the major determinant.

School related anxiety also tends to decline across transfer as shown in Figure 10. This corresponds to the data on pre- and post-transfer perceptions where adolescents report, as stated earlier, having settled in to school after the first few weeks. This decline shows a positive change in psychology for many adolescents over the transfer period. However, this type of 'transitional' anxiety should be viewed as distinct from psychosomatic anxiety which is measured with a variety of scales and is not included in the meta-analysis due to a lack of data. Studies of psychosomatic anxiety tend to show that levels remain steady for girls but decline for boys over the school transfer period (Hirsh & Rapkin, 1987). These researchers also found similar trends for depression and obsessive compulsiveness. Psychoticism increased for girls whereas phobic anxiety decreased for both genders, at each of the three transition points. Chung *et al.* (1998) found that psychological distress increased during transfer but more for girls than boys. The fact that levels of depression vary according to gender and also with age of transfer, decreasing with younger children in Grades 5 to 6 (Rudolph *et al.* 2001; Louhaus, 2004) but increasing when transferring in Grades 8 to 9 (Little & Garber, 2004) again suggests that these effects have more to do with emerging adolescence and the changing school environment than with the move to a new school.

The Structure of Transfer

Over the last few years, partly because of the National Curriculum and its age-related Key Stages, a number of Local Authorities in England have dismantled their three tier systems in favour of a single transfer at the age of eleven. In a limited number of cases attempts have been made to eliminate transfer completely by developing 'all through' 5-16 or 5-18 schools. The reasoning behind these changes has been a desire to reduce the dips in attainment on the grounds that more transitions may result in poorer academic progress, with the unstated assumption that such dips may be cumulative. In these deliberations less attention has been paid to the consequent effects on the psychological states and attitudinal dispositions of the students. It might well be argued, from the perspective of stage-environment fit theory, that the capacity of middle schools to provide a better match between the curriculum and the pupils' psychological and emotional needs should result in improved attitudes and intrinsic motivation. If so, the relatively modest hiatus in academic progress which may occur as a result of an additional transition would be a small price to pay. Some commentators have therefore suggested that a three tier system might at least slow down the decline in attitudes and lead to eventual improvements in attainment. However, apart from the Suffolk reviews (1996, 2001 and 2006) and studies by Galton and colleagues (Galton and Willcocks, 1983; Galton and Hargreaves, 2002; Hargreaves and Galton, 2002) there is little recent evidence in the UK on the differences in performance at different ages of transfer.

A study in the USA by Alspaugh (1998) addressed the relationship between the magnitude of the dips and the age of transfer in more detail. A statistically significant *academic* 'dip' was found in the transition from elementary school to middle school at 6th grade, as compared with K-8 schools that did not have a school-to-school transition at 6th grade. The dip was larger when some of the students transferring to the middle school had already undergone a transfer at an earlier age (analogous to separate infant-junior schools in the English context). Children transferring from multiple elementary schools into a single middle school (pyramid) also exhibited larger declines than those transferring between single schools (linear). Both K-8 elementary and middle school students experienced academic dips when transferring to high school at 9th grade. This was greater for the pyramid three tier schools than for the linear three tier system schools. However, both three tier systems had dips that were greater than those of the K-8 elementary students. It was also found that high school dropout rates were higher for districts with Grade 6-8 middle schools than for districts with K-8 elementary schools. This analysis therefore provides some limited evidence that the effect of frequent transfers on achievement may be cumulative.

In addition to these studies there are also two general reviews on transfer that refer to the effect of multiple transfers Juvonen (2004) considered twenty years of relevant literature and analysed existing national and international data. The author found very few studies that had compared schools with different grade configurations. Nearly all of these tended to suggest that young teenage adults did better in K-8 schools than they did under arrangements that required an additional transition to an intermediary school. Another review, undertaken by Yecke (2005), concluded that students who transfer at grade 8 did better than students who transfer at an earlier grade, and that this improvement was maintained through high school. A Canadian study by Lipps (2005) found, in contrast to the American findings, that changing schools made little difference to the adolescents' academic performance, regardless of school type. However, transferring from elementary to a middle school produced less negative emotional and behavioural impact in comparison to transfer to high schools. Considered as a whole, therefore, the North American evidence suggests that delaying the move from the elementary school helps to reduce dips at transfer. Blyth *et al.* (1983) found that the effects were greater for girls with evidence that the dips were associated with other factors such as the onset of puberty, early dating and family disruption (Simmons *et al.*1987).

Conclusions

Taken as a whole, the evidence presented here suggests that most pupils adjust fairly readily to the change of school. However, a minority do experience difficulties with consequent declines in attitudes; for a relatively small group, this period is the start of a slippery slope. Some of the worries, which give rise to their concerns initially, continue to present longer term problems and to affect their sense of wellbeing. This is particularly true of peer and teacher relationships (as discussed in greater detail earlier in this review), of attitudes to school in general and to subjects such as mathematics and science in particular. These factors, in turn, have implications for the ways that pupils regard themselves and how they take account of other people's opinions of their personality and competence. The start of secondary schooling therefore involves the negotiation and renegotiation of multiple relationships and identities (see Rudduck in Galton et al, 2003).

Most schools try to strike a balance between preserving continuity while also offering sufficient discontinuity to establish the change in their pupils' status. What schools often fail to appreciate is that the continuity-discontinuity mix is highly dependent on various factors ranging from the effects of policy formulation to the environmental conditions pertaining in feeder primary schools. This mix should therefore itself be subject to constant reappraisal in the light of changing circumstances. The evidence suggests that much of the transfer school's efforts are still concentrated on overcoming pupils' short-term concerns.

Getting a hold on the underlying factors causing these dips is more problematic. A sizeable component is doubtless attributable to changes associated with adolescence - the effects of schooling and changes in schools are probably much more modest. But some of the limitations of the evidence base also need to be acknowledged. Where research on transfer has considered possible causes, the vast bulk of the work undertaken has concentrated on the structure of schooling (as reviewed in the previous section). Much less attention has been given to alternative explanations and most of the available evidence is somewhat speculative.

Some of the factors discussed in the earlier chapter on the 'supportive' school may be relevant here as well. If we extrapolate from that evidence it seems possible that secondary schools are experienced by young people as somehow looser and less 'connected' than their primary equivalents. Clearly relationships with teachers also differ; whereas in the primary school pupils mostly form bonds with a single teacher, at the middle and secondary stages they must relate to a significantly larger number of staff, some of whom may not be perceived as entirely congenial. Relationships with peers also change as pupils progress through school with friendship networks becoming larger and more extended; some transitions may involve a diminution in the perceived levels of support as friendship groups are broken up and only partially re-formed. Dissatisfaction with the general 'school experience' also becomes more prominent and is also voiced more frequently. The 'thinking small' initiatives outlined earlier have been prompted in part by worries about transfer between institutions but also by continuing concerns relating to the 'pupil experience' as they progress through the latter stages of secondary schooling.

CHAPTER SIX

CHANGES IN ATTITUDES OVER TIME

Whilst long-run trends in academic attainment have been frequently measured and extensively reported, we were able to identify very little research tracking changes in young people's attitudes and experiences towards their schools and education over significant periods of a decade or more. We did, however, find two nationally representative studies, which are of some interest.

The first is based on data obtained from the bi-annual Youth Cohort Study of England and Wales and the Scottish School Leavers Surveys and covers the period 1984-2000 (Croxford, 2007). These surveys asked young people to look back on their school experiences and to report on their perceptions. Clearly, by the time these young people had left school they were a little older than the target group for this review but the findings are nonetheless of interest.

Young people were asked to respond to three statements about schooling. The evidence generally supports the view that, in terms at least of these three measures, young people became a bit more positive about their schooling over the period covered by the surveys (tables not shown). In 1984 just under 60% felt that their school 'had done little to prepare (them) for life after school'; by the turn of the century this had fallen to just over a third (i.e. an improvement in attitudes). Just over 50% felt that school had 'helped give (them) the confidence to make decisions'; again this rose to somewhere around 70%. Similarly, during the 1980s just over half felt that school had 'taught (them) things which would be useful in a job'; this too rose to around 70% (tables not shown).

Croxford (2007) has grouped all the items together with a view to exploring the extent to which they were suggestive of trends in overall attitudes towards school. These results are displayed in Figure 11 below which indicates that there was a general upward movement in the level of positive responses in all three participating countries. The average number of positive responses given rose over this fifteen-year period from somewhere around 1.5 to around 2.0 positive responses per student.

Figure 11: Average Number of Positive Responses to Schooling Items 1984-1999

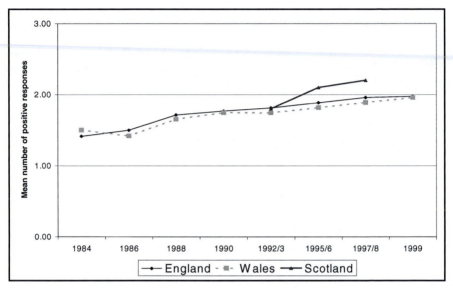

Source: Croxford (2007)

The Health Behaviour in School-Aged Children (HBSC) surveys, sponsored by the World Health Organisation, relate to a later period although they were first started in the 1980s. Whilst England was involved at that time, regrettably it dropped out of a subsequent sweep and did not participate again until 1997/1998. Since that time there have been two further surveys which bring the picture over the last decade up to date (Currie et al, 2000; Currie et al, 2004; Currie et al, 2008). It should be noted, however, that there are some complications in comparing the surveys over time as: each survey has been reported separately and no formal time-series have been published; the numbers of participating countries has also grown; and the wording of questions has sometimes varied from one survey to the next.

Liking School

Table 5 has been compiled by bringing together data contained in three separate reports. It provides evidence of the extent to which young people in England reported that they 'liked' school. The wording here was comparable so comparisons over time are appropriate. The table also shows the average responses of young people across the different HBSC countries participating in the study as a whole. Interpretation is complicated, however, by the fact that there seems to have been a dip in responses amongst the 2001/2002 English respondents; this did not affect the whole HBSC sample, however in other countries, to anywhere near the same extent.

Comparing the 1997/1998 responses with those in 2005/2006 young people in England were generally more satisfied in the most recent survey. Over half of both 11 year old boys and girls liked school. Furthermore, although the proportions dropped to around a third and a quarter of 13 and 15 year olds respectively, this finding appears to hold true, regardless of which age-group is being considered. The upwards shift is consistent with the sort of responses noted earlier in relation to Figure 7.

Table 5: Young people's reports of how much they liked school

11 Year Olds	1997/1998 'like school a lot' (%)	2001/2002 'like school a lot' (%)	2005/2006 'like school a lot (%)
English Boys	37	25	56
English Girls	49	28	52
HBSC Boys	30	30	33
HBSC Girls	39	38	43
13 Year Olds			
English Boys	19	14	31
English Girls	24	16	33
HBSC Boys	17	17	22
HBSC Girls	24	22	27
15 Year Olds			
English Boys	15	15	26
English Girls	16	15	24
HBSC Boys	14	15	18
HBSC Girls	18	17	22

Source: HBSC Surveys

Table 6: Young people's perceptions of their own school performance

11 Year Olds	1997/1998 Perceived as 'very good' (%)	2001/2002 Perceived as 'good/very good' (%)	2005/2006 Perceived as 'good/very good' (%)
English Boys	21	61	76
English Girls	26	71	80
HBSC Boys	18	66	70
HBSCGirls	22	72	77
13 Year Olds			
English Boys	16	58	68
English Girls	18	65	75
HBSCBoys	12	56	60
HBSCGirls	17	62	66
15 Year Olds			
English Boys	15	57	66
English Girls	17	64	67
HBSCBoys	11	50	53
HBSCGirls	13	56	59

Source: HBSC Surveys

Unfortunately, responses across the three surveys are not readily comparable in relation to young people's perceptions of their own school performance because of the different way in which the earlier survey was worded. In 1997/98 respondents were asked to rate their own achievement; in the later surveys they were asked to report what, in their opinion, their 'class teacher(s) thought about their school performance' compared with their classmates.

In the 2005/2006 survey over three quarters of 11 year olds believed that their teachers thought their performance was 'good' or 'very good' (see Table 6). Again, responses amongst 13 and 15 year olds were less favourable. There appears to have been a small shift in an upward direction between the 2001/2002 survey and the 2005/2006 one, which was mirrored, albeit to a lesser extent, in the responses of the HBSC sample as well.

Peer support

The evidence in relation to peer support is generally consistent with these suggestions of upward trends. The wording here is comparable across the three surveys. In the latest 2005/2006 HBSC survey roughly four fifths of 11 year olds reported that they found their peers 'kind and helpful' whilst around two thirds of 13 and 15 year olds felt the same (see Table 7).

Table 7: Young people's perceptions of levels of peer support

11 Year Olds	1997/1998 Peers 'kind & helpful' (%)	2001/2002 Peers 'kind & helpful' (%)	2005/2006 Peers 'kind & helpful' (%)
English Boys	55	45	79
English Girls	62	56	84
HBSC Boys	62	70	69
HBSC Girls	63	72	71
13 Year Olds			
English Boys	43	34	66
English Girls	48	42	72
HBSC Boys	54	61	62
HBSC Girls	57	62	63
15 Year Olds			
English Boys	40	36	68
English Girls	48	47	72
HBSC Boys	53	58	61
HBSC Girls	56	60	63

Source: HBSC Surveys

The percentages replying positively amongst the English sample in the 1997/1998 and 2001/2002 surveys were reasonably similar. However, there was a striking upward shift in the responses of the English samples between the 2001/2002 survey and that conducted in 2005/2006; roughly thirty per cent more pupils in each age group and of both sexes reported more favourable experiences in relation to their peers' attitudes and behaviour. These shifts of perception are also striking when compared to the relatively stable position prevailing across the whole HBSC sample over the same time-frame. Whilst there was undoubtedly more emphasis in schools on wellbeing issues during the early 2000s we do not have a clear explanation for the size of the changes the surveys indicate.

Feeling pressured

Quite high proportions of English young people felt that they were pressured by their schoolwork although the different nature of the question reported in the earliest survey needs to be noted (see Table 8). In the 2005/2006 survey around four out of ten young people felt 'some' or 'a lot of' pressure. These proportions rose to roughly half amongst 13 year olds. English 15 year olds felt especially pressured with around two thirds reporting these sorts of feelings. In contrast to the other items reported in earlier tables, there was a quite sizeable gap between their reports and those of their HBSC counterparts, especially amongst the oldest age-group; 60% of English 15 year old boys felt pressured compared with 40% of the HBSC sample whilst for girls the percentages were 70% and 49% respectively.

Table 8: Young people's perceptions of feeling pressured by schoolwork

11 Year Olds	1997/1998 Feel a lot of pressure (%)	2001/2002 Feel some/lot of pressure (%)	2005/2006 Feel some/lot of pressure (%)
English Boys	9	40	43
English Girls	6	29	37
HBSC Boys	7	27	24
HBSC Girls	6	23	27
13 Year Olds			
English Boys	10	40	48
English Girls	10	41	48
HBSC Boys	9	34	35
HBSC Girls	8	37	38
15 Year Olds			
English Boys	23	59	60
English Girls	36	70	70
HBSC Boys	11	41	40
HBSC Girls	14	48	49

Source: HBSC Surveys

Life Satisfaction

The relationships between these feelings about school and more general feelings of 'life satisfaction' have already been mentioned although they were not particularly strong. However, they do not appear to have spilled over into English young people's more general feelings about life (see Table 9). Very high proportions of them (between eight and nine out of ten) reported 'medium' or 'high' 'life satisfaction'. These proportions seemed relatively stable when compared with the position in 2001/2002 but again difficulties in comparing responses from the earlier and later surveys need to be noted.

Their responses were also fairly comparable to those of their HBSC counterparts where similarly high proportions of both boys and girls reported feeling satisfied. In passing we note that these figures are not dissimilar to those reported for a slightly older sample in a recent survey by DEFRA (2007). Amongst 16-24 year olds responding to a ten point scale ranging from 'extremely dissatisfied' to 'extremely satisfied', 84% gave positive responses of 6 or above (i.e. the same cut-off point as that used in the HBSC survey).

Table 9: Young people's reports of their 'life satisfaction'

	1997/1998 'not feeling low'	2001/2002 'medium/high' life satisfaction	2005/2006 'medium/high' life satisfaction
11 Year Olds	(%)	(%)	(%)
English Boys	27	87	88
English Girls	27	82	88
HBSC Boys	21	88	88
HBSC Girls	26	87	87
13 Year Olds			
English Boys	33	88	87
English Girls	25	81	81
HBSC Boys	33	87	87
HBSC Girls	21	83	82
15 Year Olds			
English Boys	24	85	89
English Girls	40	78	79
HBSC Boys	23	85	85
HBSC Girls	39	77	78

Conclusions

The evidence on changes in young people's attitudes towards school over time is fairly sparse and only rarely covers more than a decade. The data we have been able to assemble here nonetheless suggest that there has been no obvious trend in a downwards direction – attitudes do not appear to have got worse in recent years. There are also some signs that there may have been modest improvements. In recent years adolescents appear to have liked school a bit more, been a little more inclined to believe that their teachers rated their performance highly and been more likely to find their peers supportive.   Substantial groups felt pressured by their schoolwork (in particular 15 year olds, for whom external exams will have loomed large and especially 15 year-old girls) but whether there was a clear trend towards feeling more pressured over time is not clear. Changes in attitudes, however, do not appear to have unduly influenced reports of 'life satisfaction' where levels have remained fairly constant in recent years.

CHAPTER SEVEN

VULNERABLE GROUPS, BULLYING AND EXCLUSION

We reported earlier that somewhere over one in ten young people in the 11-15 age-group had a clinically recognizable 'mental disorder'; these were predominantly of a conduct or emotional nature although small proportions (around one per cent or fewer) had 'hyperkinetic' and other 'less common' disorders (Parry-Langdon, 2004). As we have also suggested, a larger group of young people may well experience periods when there is some disruption to their emotional wellbeing. The evidence on co-morbidity indicates that one in five of children diagnosed with a disorder had at least one other disorder, the most common combinations being conduct and emotional disorders and conduct and hyperkinetic disorders (ONS, 2005).

The greater majority of children with multiple disorders were male, reflecting the high proportion of children with conduct disorders in this age-group. Children suffering from more than one disorder were also at greater risk of suffering more serious problems: just under two thirds of those with multiple disorders were also behind in their intellectual development, compared to around half of those with a single disorder whilst children with multiple disorders accounted for approximately one third of those using specialist mental health services.

Whilst some of these conditions are unlikely to be directly affected by young people's educational experiences others may well be - although causal directions are again difficult to disentangle, there is clearly some conjunction. As Bradshaw and colleagues (2004: 38) remind us, 'Schools can and do make a (varying) difference to children and young people's educational attainment and ultimately their life chances'. The degree to which the same factors appear to be associated with low educational achievement as well as poor wellbeing outcomes is striking.

Links with background factors affecting educational achievement

'Family affluence' seems to have some effects on wellbeing and to serve as a protective factor. The HBSC studies, for example, report that 'higher levels of socioeconomic status, as measured by family affluence, were associated with positive health outcomes in both genders and in almost all countries' (Currie et al, 2008: 178). They also found a strikingly 'consistent association' between 'family affluence' and life satisfaction'. 'In all but one country, those from more affluent families (were) significantly more likely to report high levels of life satisfaction' (*op cit*: 177). The same study additionally reports that, in many countries (although not all) students from more affluent families 'were more likely …. to like school a lot' and to enjoy higher levels of peer support. It should be noted, however, that these were tendencies – none of the relationships was particularly strong.

Conversely, social disadvantage seems, in many circumstances, to represent some kind of a risk factor. The links between types of disorder and gender have already been noted. Of the various disorders already discussed boys were much more likely to have conduct and hyperkinetic disorders whilst girls *were* over-represented in terms of emotional problems. But there were also other notable correlates amongst which various aspects of socio-economic background loom large. The Office for National Statistics (2005) reports that children with mental health problems were more likely:

- to live in households with lower incomes;
- to live in rented accommodation;
- to have parents neither of whom worked;
- to have parents who worked in routine/semi-routine jobs as opposed to professional ones;
- to have parents with few if any educational qualifications; and
- to suffer poor physical health.

The strength of these relationships varied but, in every case, they were quite substantial. Family make-up also appears to impact on the mental health of young people. Problems were reported to be more than twice as prevalent amongst children from single parent families compared to married couples whilst their prevalence in reconstituted families (where stepchildren were present) was also greater.

So-called 'looked after' children, brought up in local authority care, seem to be particularly at risk of poor mental health. The ONS (2003) reported that in the 5-17 age-group 45% of those in the looked after group had a mental health disorder compared with just ten per cent from other types of household.

Evidence on the patterning of mental health problems amongst young black and ethnic minority groups is less secure than that for the white population because sample sizes have tended to be small; language barriers may also have intruded in instances where English was not the first language. The ONS reports that children from Indian families had a lower reported rate of mental health problems than other groups and that all non-white groups had a low rate of hyperkinetic disorders (BMA, 2003). Interestingly, from the point of view of the earlier discussion of evidence on school experiences, no significant variations were found in the incidence of problems between England, Scotland and Wales although we encountered a suggestion that their prevalence might be a little higher in Northern Ireland, possibly owing to that country's troubles over the last three decades (Northern Ireland, 2005).

Around 10% of pupils appear to have severe problems of adjustment at transfer. Most of these are likely to have special needs or to have underperformed relative to their assessed potential in the feeder school. They are likely to be male (ILEA 1986; Muldoon 2005; Evangelou *et al,* 2008). Children with learning difficulties worried more about friendships and being bullied and had a greater chance of being victims (McMaugh & Debus, 1999; Evangelou *et al.*2008). They had, in part as a consequence of these negative feelings, lower self-esteem (Forgan & Vaughn, 2000; Jindal-Snape & Foggie, 2008). Their relationships with teachers were also less successful (Feeney & Best, 1997) perhaps, as Galton and MacBeath (2008) have observed, because these children tend to have less contact with their class teacher, being assigned for most of the lesson to the care of a classroom assistant.   Minority ethnic groups may also experience problems. Having only a small number of children of similar ethnicity undertaking transfer to a particular school seems to increase concerns, including those of bullying and difficulties in making (and maintaining) friendships which can result in a higher probability of disengagement (Benner & Graham, 2007). Asian children, however, appear less susceptible to a loss of interest in education than other ethnic groups (Graham & Hill, 2003).

The incidence of bullying

The issue of bullying is a particularly important one in terms of mental health. *The Good Childhood Inquiry*, for example, reports that young people in their large sample commonly mentioned bullying as a source of unhappiness (Pople, 2009). Much bullying takes place at school where young people are thrown together although some can occur outside school as well. It can take a variety of forms including both physical attacks and activities such as name calling which are calculated to undermine psychological wellbeing.

Being bullied repeatedly at school can constitute a serious health risk and children who are frequently bullied are more likely than others to report comparatively low levels of mental health (Rigby, 2005). Although causal links can be difficult to establish, as Craig and Harel (2004) argue, 'repeated bullying consolidates the power relations between bullies and their victims: the former gain power and the latter lose it'.

A number of mental health consequences seem to stem from being bullied. For example, Craig (1998) reports that victims are more likely to be depressed than other young people; Boulton and Underwood (1992) note lower self-esteem and a higher incidence of perceived loneliness; whilst Smith and Sharpe (1994) along with Olweus (1991 and 1994) detect more anxiety and insecurity amongst those who have been bullied.

The two most recent HBSC surveys have both explored the incidence of bullying. Those surveyed were asked to say how often they had been bullied in the past couple of months; Table 10 below reports on those who said that it happened 'two or three times a month', 'about once a week' or 'several times a week'. Both surveys indicate that the experience of being bullied was quite prevalent amongst English adolescents although it declined a little amongst the older age-groups. In both the 11 and 13 year old samples, however, at least one in ten boys and girls reported being bullied at least twice in the past couple of months. Boys were slightly more exposed to this experience than girls. English adolescents, however, were somewhat less likely to report being bullied than their counterparts across all the countries participating in the HBSC surveys.

Table 10: Young people's reports of the experience of being bullied at least twice in the past couple of months

11 Year Olds	2001/2002 Been bullied at least twice (%)	2005/2006 Been bullied at least twice (%)
English Boys	17	11
English Girls	13	9
HBSC Boys	16	16
HBSC Girls	13	13
13 Year Olds		
English Boys	14	12
English Girls	14	9
HBSC Boys	15	15
HBSC Girls	12	13
15 Year Olds		
English Boys	7	9
English Girls	11	8
HBSC Boys	11	11
HBSC Girls	8	8

Source: HBSC Surveys

Similar estimates emerge from other studies in the UK. Smith and Shu (2000), for example, report that about one in eight young people said they had been bullied more than once or twice in the previous six months. A study of young people in East London provides similar estimates for Year 9 pupils saying they had been 'bullied this term'. However, in this same study, up to a quarter of Year 7 pupils reported that they had been bullied (Institute of Community Health Sciences, 2003: 74). The authors of this study note, in passing, that 'it may be that adolescents under-report having been bullied, as a much higher percentage of pupils had recently experienced behavior that might be considered bullying'. Networks of social support (especially from fellow pupils) can provide some protection against the negative effects of being victimized (Rigby, 2002; Hartup and Abecassis, 2004).

Those who bully may themselves be at some risk, especially in relation to the incidence of depression as well as other potentially detrimental mental health outcomes (Farrington, 1993; Volk et al, 2006). In the two HBSC surveys only small percentages of young people reported bullying others on a regular basis (see Table 11 below). Boys were roughly twice as likely to report doing so as girls. The incidence of this kind of behaviour in the English sample, however, was considerably lower than for the HBSC countries as a whole.

Table 11: Young people's reports of bullying others at school at least twice in the past couple of months

11 Year Olds	2001/2002 Bullied others at least twice(%)	2005/2006 Bullied others at least twice(%)
English Boys	7	4
English Girls	3	2
HBSC Boys	12	12
HBSC Girls	6	6
13 Year Olds		
English Boys	8	8
English Girls	5	5
HBSC Boys	16	15
HBSC Girls	8	9
15 Year Olds		
English Boys	11	10
English Girls	4	6
HBSC Boys	18	16
HBSC Girls	8	7

Source: HBSC Surveys

Table 12: Overlap between fighting, bullying and being bullied

Behaviour	(%)
No aggressive behavior	35
Victimisation	10
Fighting	14
Bullying	8
Fighting and bullying	9
Fighting or bullying and victimisation	24
Total	100

Source: Craig and Harel, 2004, Figure 3.39

A further analysis from the HBSC surveys provides some interesting insights into the incidence of fighting, bullying and being bullied. As Craig and Harel (2004: 143) note, peer aggression and victimization are recognized as 'significant obstacles to healthy educational, social and emotional adjustment'. There is often a considerable overlap between the two activities (see Table 12). The largest group of young people (35%) in the HBSC survey were not engaged in any kind of aggressive behaviour whilst a further group (10%) reported that they were just victims. However, the second largest group in the table (24%) was involved in each, reporting both that they fought or bullied and that they were also victimized.

It is difficult to establish whether there have been changes in how vulnerable children are perceived and responded to in school or whether conditions have improved over time. One measure would be how schools have responded to bullying and there has, indeed, been a major policy focus on reducing bullying in schools (Smith 2003). Smith and Shu (2000), for example, reported some decrease in the numbers of children being bullied and an increase in the rates of reporting of bullying, both of which suggest that practice has been developed and that the importance of anti-bullying work has been emphasized. Nonetheless, quite sizeable differences between schools appear to persist (McLaughlin et al, 2005).

Exclusion from School

Exclusion from school matters for at least three reasons: first because it affects the life chances of the young people who are excluded; second, because there is evidence that the group of young people most excluded are those with special needs, particularly of an emotional and behavioural kind; and third, because connection to school can be a protective factor (Smith 2006). Pupils with special educational needs have suffered disproportionately from these developments (Warnock, 2005). Parsons and colleagues (2001) have shown that this group is up to nine times more likely to be excluded from school. Boys have also been up to four times more likely to be excluded than girls. Those excluded from school also have much poorer prognoses for their long-term development (Bradshaw et al, 2004).

Figure 12 below covers the better part of two decades. It shows a large increase in the numbers of pupils that were permanently excluded from primary, secondary and special schools.

Figure 12: Number of Permanent Exclusions in English Schools 1990/91-2006/07 broken down by school type

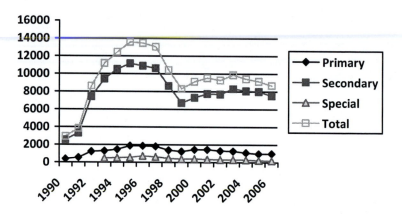

Source: National Statistics, DCSF 14/2008, 24 June 2008

The greater majority (over 80%) of such exclusions were from secondary schools (Cooper et al, 2000). However, what is perhaps most notable about the evidence is the sharp rise in exclusions in schools of all kinds during the early 1990s; in secondary schools this amounted to a more than four-fold increase. Since that time the numbers of permanent exclusions have fallen to around 8,000 a year. Nonetheless, the rate of exclusion in 2007 in secondary schools was well over three times as high as that which prevailed some two decades earlier whilst levels in primary schools were also higher than before. Research by Stirling (1992, 1996) suggests that the rate of unofficial exclusions has also increased alongside the official one.

It is not clear precisely what factors have produced the changes but they are likely to have been linked, in some way, to the policy changes initiated by the 1988 Education Reform Act which included: the introduction of a national curriculum; more explicit competition between schools; and an element of choice for parents about which school their child might attend. Standardised testing of academic achievement was introduced a couple of years later and subsequently so-called league tables of school performance. In the process expectations about schools' performance (and the management of that performance) have been ramped up with consequences for those less able (or suited) to meet the more demanding yardsticks of assessment. Such developments may have increased the pressure on schools to be somewhat less tolerant of pupils with emotional and behavioural difficulties and, in some cases, to take a more punitive stance (Parsons, 2005). At the same time expectations of young people's behavior may have risen, as they have for teachers. Policy initiatives to increase the proportions of pupils educated in mainstream schools may also have exacerbated the pressures on schools.

Conclusions

Around ten per cent of adolescents appear to have mental disorders of one kind or another. Pupils with special educational needs are disproportionately represented in this group. Many of the correlates of educational achievement related to young people's backgrounds (such as parental socio-economic status and education, household composition and so on) also seem to be associated with poorer mental health outcomes. How far these two groups overlap, however, is not yet entirely clear. There is undoubtedly a group which experiences both low educational achievement *and* poor mental health outcomes; adolescents who do not perform well at school in academic terms seem more likely to be vulnerable in terms of wellbeing. However, the degree of overlap between the two groups and questions of causal direction remains largely unclear. Some young people appear to have reasonable levels of wellbeing despite poor academic achievement.

Around ten per cent of young people report that they have been subject to bullying; when this occurs repeatedly, young people's feelings of wellbeing undoubtedly suffer. Over the last two decades the rate of exclusions from schools has risen considerably as a result of changes in national policies and schools' approaches. Young people who are vulnerable in terms of mental health seem to be more at risk of being permanently excluded from school.

CHAPTER EIGHT

WELLBEING IN AN INTERNATIONAL CONTEXT

England's position in international 'league tables' has provoked a good deal of negative comment (see discussion of Table 2 earlier). As is often the case, however, the disaggregated data present a more complex picture. The evidence in Table 13 below compares England's position on five variables related to wellbeing with that of some 40 other countries that participated in the most recent HBSC 2005/2006 survey. To simplify comparisons (and to avoid suggestions of undue precision) the data have been summarized in terms of four quartiles (based on ranking positions).

There are some surprises. English young people appear to like school, at least relative to most of their international counterparts. In five out of the six comparison groups their responses placed them in the top quartile of favourable responses; in brief, they liked school more than their counterparts in at least three quarters of the other participating countries. Only 15 year old girls were less enthusiastic but even their responses provided an upper quartile ranking, meaning that they were more favourably disposed than half the other countries.

English young people's perceptions of their own performance were also favourable (see Table 13). Two out of the six groups were in the top quartile and the remaining four were located in the upper quartile. Similarly, responses to relationships with peers were encouraging with five out of six groups placed in the upper quartile and one in the top quartile.

These generally positive responses need to be contrasted, however, with the overwhelmingly negative responses of English young people to the question about the pressures of schoolwork (see Table 13). The responses of all six groups placed them firmly in the bottom quartile (amongst the quarter of countries with the least favourable responses on this item). English young people, in short, seem to have felt very pressured indeed - in only two countries out of some 40 did their counterparts appear to have had less favourable reactions.

Table 13: England's Rankings (by Quartile) in the HBSC Survey in 2005/06

Area of Wellbeing	Girls 11	Boys 11	Girls 13	Boys 13	Girls 15	Boys 15
Liking school 'a lot'	Top	Top	Top	Top	Upper	Top
Perceiving own performance as 'good/very good'	Upper	Upper	Top	Upper	Upper	Top
Finding peers 'kind and helpful'	Top	Upper	Upper	Upper	Upper	Upper
Feeling pressured by schoolwork*	Bottom	Bottom	Bottom	Bottom	Bottom	Bottom
Reporting medium/high life satisfaction	Upper	Upper	Lower	Lower	Upper	Top

Note: for the purposes of presentation the group of countries where pupils felt *least* pressured has been described as being in the top quartile.

Some of these responses to school experiences appear to have influenced young people's reports of broader 'life satisfaction' although here the comparative picture is a little more mixed. The responses of one group (15 year old boys) placed them in the top quartile, three were in the upper quartile (11 year old boys and girls and 15 year old girls) whilst two were in the lower quartile (13 year old boys and girls).

Trends over time

Comparing responses to the HBSC surveys over time presents some difficulties, not least because the number of participating countries has increased considerably over the last decade. Consequently changes in ranking over time need to be considered with some care and hedged with caveats. The pattern of responses on the four key school variables is nonetheless of some interest.

The ways in which English young people's attitudes to school have fluctuated over time has already been noted. In the 1997/1998 survey the profile of their responses about liking school placed them firmly in the upper quartile of participating countries (table not shown). In the 2001/2002 survey, however, they fell into or near the bottom quartile before bouncing back in the 2005/2006 survey into the top quartile. Perceptions of their own school performance followed a similar, although not so marked, pattern. An upper quartile placing in the first (1997/1998) survey dipped in the second (2001/2002) before returning to earlier levels in the third (2005/2006).

The change over time in young people's responses about the extent to which their peers were 'kind and helpful' is particularly striking. In the first survey the English responses hovered around the borderline for the bottom quartile whilst, in the second, they collapsed completely (table not shown); England was at the bottom and these responses will undoubtedly have impacted very significantly on the UNICEF table reported earlier. In the latest survey, however, the English position was much more favourable with the responses producing an upper quartile ranking. Whether this change was directly linked to changes in policy and practice is unclear.

There is one area, however, in which the responses have remained stable over time. In each of the three surveys English adolescents have claimed to feel very pressured by the demands of schoolwork and, in each case, their replies have placed them firmly in the bottom quartile (table not shown). The consistency with which this finding has stood up over time is notable.

International Comparisons

Another way of gaining some purchase on the responses of English adolescents is to compare them with some of their international counterparts. Obviously, with some 40 countries represented in the HBSC surveys, a very considerable number of comparisons are potentially possible. For heuristic purposes we have adopted a more limited sub-set of countries, looking broadly at three groups. The first is composed of England's near neighbours (Ireland, Scotland and Wales) whose educational systems, in many respects, are closely comparable. The second group was made up of England's cross-Channel partners (the Flemish part of Belgium, Denmark and the Netherlands), whilst the third comprised Nordic countries (Finland, Norway and Sweden) which have topped various international tables on a fairly regular basis.

Generally speaking, reported levels of 'life satisfaction' in both the
cross-Channel and Nordic groups were high (see Table 14). In both cases
all six groups of boys and girls were located in the top or upper quartile.
Both groups of countries also outstripped the responses of English
adolescents by some distance. The group comprising the remainder of the
UK and Ireland was more closely comparable to the English case although
nonetheless varied. Responses in Ireland were more favourable than in
England but both Scotland and Wales had poorer profiles, in the latter
case, to quite a considerable degree.

Table 14: Reported Levels of 'Life Satisfaction' in Selected Countries

Country	Girls 11	Boys 11	Girls 13	Boys 13	Girls 15	Boys 15
England	Upper	Upper	Lower	Lower	Upper	Top
Ireland	Top	Top	Top	Upper	Lower	Upper
Scotland	Lower	Upper	Lower	Upper	Lower	Upper
Wales	Bottom	Bottom	Bottom	Lower	Bottom	Upper
Belgium (Flemish)	Top	Upper	Top	Top	Top	Top
Denmark	Upper	Top	Top	Top	Top	Top
Netherlands	Top	Top	Top	Top	Top	Top
Finland	Top	Top	Top	Top	Top	Top
Norway	Upper	Upper	Upper	Upper	Upper	Upper
Sweden	Top	Top	Lower	Top	Upper	Top

Source: HBSC Survey 2005/2006

We had anticipated that young people in the cross-Channel and Nordic
countries would be more favourably disposed to school than their English
counterparts. The survey results, however, suggest a more complicated
picture (see Table 15); there was considerable variation amongst both
groups. Young people in England were inclined to like school as much as
in most of the other countries. Their counterparts in the Netherlands
clearly liked school as well with three of the groups appearing in the top
quartile and the other three in the upper quartile. On the other hand a more
mixed picture emerged in Denmark and Belgium with responses split
equally between the upper and lower quartiles. Norwegian youngsters

undoubtedly 'liked' school to a similar or greater extent than England and the Netherlands but, somewhat surprisingly, those in Finland and Sweden did not. The Swedish picture was mixed with none of the groups featuring in the top quartile and the two groups of 15 year-old boys and girls appearing in the bottom quartile. Still more surprisingly, Finnish youngsters appeared particularly antipathetic to school – no fewer than five of the six groups featured in the bottom quartile. Indeed, in general terms, roughly twice as many English young people liked school as their Finnish peers (table not shown).

Table 15: Reported Levels of 'Liking School' in Selected Countries

Country	Girls 11	Boys 11	Girls 13	Boys 13	Girls 15	Boys 15
England	Top	Top	Top	Top	Upper	Top
Ireland	Bottom	Bottom	Top	Upper	Upper	Lower
Scotland	Upper	Upper	Lower	Upper	Lower	Lower
Wales	Lower	Lower	Lower	Lower	Lower	Upper
Belgium (Flemish)	Lower	Upper	Upper	Upper	Lower	Lower
Denmark	Upper	Lower	Lower	Upper	Lower	Upper
Netherlands	Upper	Upper	Top	Top	Top	Upper
Finland	Bottom	Bottom	Lower	Bottom	Bottom	Bottom
Norway	Top	Top	Top	Top	Top	Top
Sweden	Lower	Upper	Lower	Upper	Bottom	Bottom

Source: HBSC Survey 2005/2006

English young people perceived their own academic performance as strong in comparison with the ways in which their international counterparts viewed themselves. Two of the six English groups featured in the top quartile whilst the remaining four all fell into the upper quartile (see Table 16). This profile was, broadly speaking, matched by the Irish and Welsh but not Scottish youngsters. Self perceptions were uniformly lower in the cross-Channel countries, especially in the cases of Belgium and the Netherlands. The picture in the Nordic countries was similarly mixed – only Swedish young people appeared to rate themselves as highly as the English.

Table 16: Reported Self-Perceptions of 'Academic Performance' in Selected Countries

Country	Girls 11	Boys 11	Girls 13	Boys 13	Girls 15	Boys 15
England	Upper	Upper	Top	Upper	Upper	Top
Ireland	Top	Upper	Top	Upper	Top	Top
Scotland	Lower	Lower	Upper	Upper	Upper	Upper
Wales	Upper	Upper	Upper	Top	Top	Top
Belgium (Flemish)	Bottom	Lower	Bottom	Bottom	Bottom	Bottom
Denmark	Top	Top	Lower	Upper	Lower	Lower
Netherlands	Lower	Lower	Upper	Lower	Lower	Lower
Finland	Lower	Lower	Lower	Upper	Lower	Lower
Norway	Lower	Top	Lower	Lower	Lower	Lower
Sweden	Upper	Upper	Upper	Top	Upper	Upper

Source: HBSC Survey 2005/2006

Both the Nordic and cross-Channel countries had high proportions of their young people perceiving their peers as 'kind and helpful' (see Table 17). Amongst the Nordic countries, all or most of the six groups in Norway and Sweden fell into the top quartile whilst the Finnish picture was also favourable. The position in the cross-Channel countries was similar with young people in Denmark and the Netherlands reporting in particularly positive terms. English adolescents also featured in the upper quartile without quite matching these two groups. The patterns in the other parts of the UK and Ireland were more mixed however, with young people in Wales almost uniformly appearing in the lower quartile.

Table 17: Perceptions of Peers as 'Kind and Helpful' in Selected Countries

Country	Girls 11	Boys 11	Girls 13	Boys 13	Girls 15	Boys 15
England	Top	Upper	Upper	Upper	Upper	Upper
Ireland	Top	Upper	Upper	Lower	Upper	Lower
Scotland	Top	Top	Upper	Upper	Lower	Lower
Wales	Lower	Lower	Lower	Bottom	Lower	Lower
Belgium (Flemish)	Top	Top	Top	Upper	Upper	Upper
Denmark	Top	Top	Top	Top	Top	Top
Netherlands	Top	Upper	Top	Top	Top	Top
Finland	Upper	Upper	Upper	Upper	Upper	Upper
Norway	Top	Top	Top	Top	Top	Top
Sweden	Top	Top	Top	Top	Upper	Top

Source: HBSC Survey 2005/2006

In short, in relation to three of the four school variables reported here, responses from English young people compared favourably with most of their cross-Channel and Nordic counterparts. With respect to feeling 'pressured by schoolwork', however, there were some stark differences (see Table 18).

Table 18: Perceptions of Feeling 'Pressured by Schoolwork' in Selected Countries

Country	Girls 11	Boys 11	Girls 13	Boys 13	Girls 15	Boys 15
England	Bottom	Bottom	Bottom	Bottom	Bottom	Bottom
Ireland	Upper	Upper	Lower	Lower	Lower	Lower
Scotland	Upper	Upper	Top	Top	Upper	Upper
Wales	Lower	Lower	Upper	Lower	Bottom	Bottom
Belgium (Flemish)	Lower	Top	Upper	Top	Top	Top
Denmark	Upper	Lower	Upper	Upper	Upper	Upper
Netherlands	Top	Top	Top	Top	Top	Top
Finland	Lower	Bottom	Upper	Lower	Lower	Lower
Norway	Top	Upper	Upper	Upper	Lower	Lower
Sweden	Top	Top	Top	Top	Bottom	Lower

Source: HBSC Survey 2005/2006

Note: for the purposes of presentation the group of countries where pupils felt *least* pressured has been described as being in the top quartile.

Each of the six English groups featured in the bottom quartile and clearly, in comparative terms, saw themselves as very pressured. In the Netherlands, by contrast, every group appeared in the top quartile. The patterns in Belgium and Denmark were also relatively favourable with most groups falling into the upper or top quartiles. The Nordic countries presented a more varied picture however. The responses of the 11 and 13 year old groups in Norway and Sweden were concentrated in the upper or top quartiles but were appreciably lower amongst their 15 year olds. The Finnish case was notably different, with five of the six groups located in the lower or even bottom quartiles.

Conclusions

The responses of English young people to questions about their degree of 'life satisfaction' present a mixed picture; four of the six age groups (boys and girls aged 11 and 15) gave responses which placed them in at least the upper quartile whilst in two cases they fell into the lower quartile (boys and girls aged 13). Reports of their school experiences, however, compared favourably in most respects with those of their international counterparts in the HBSC surveys. They emerged, in comparative terms, as mostly liking school, finding their peers kind and helpful and believing that their teachers judged them to be performing well academically. But they also felt markedly more pressured by their schoolwork than their peers from other countries, a situation which has held true for the last decade.

The responses of English young people to questions about their school experiences also compared favourably with most of their cross-Channel and Nordic counterparts. However, there were also some surprises here. Finnish and Swedish adolescents, for example, appeared not to like school to the same extent as English 11-15 year olds; Dutch youngsters did not believe their academic performance was rated well by their teachers; and, interestingly, most of the Finnish groups felt pressured by their schoolwork, although not to the same extent as their English peers.

CHAPTER NINE

WELLBEING AND THE INFLUENCE
OF THE SCHOOL

Research on school effectiveness attempts to establish the distinctive and unique contribution that schools make to young people's development. This tradition of research stretches back to the mid-sixties and the Coleman (1966) and Plowden (1967) Reports in the USA and UK respectively. Then, after a lull that lasted the better part of a decade, it was given renewed impetus by Rutter and colleagues' (1979) pioneering study of 12 inner London schools. Since then the number of studies has increased still further.

The main messages of the large body of work that now exists on school effectiveness may be briefly summarised. The research has established both that schools make *some* difference to their pupils' achievements and has, in addition, identified some of the school-related factors that contribute to differential outcomes. Studies typically estimate that the school component of variations in pupils' achievements varies from 8-15% of the total variance (see Teddlie and Reynolds, 2000 for a summary). Attending a so-called 'more effective' school as opposed to a 'less effective' one seems to boost a pupil's performance by about a grade in each of three or four exam subjects. Differences between primary schools in effectiveness seem to be a little larger than differences between secondaries. And schools which do well in terms of one cognitive outcome have tended to perform better in relation to others.

Rutter's conclusions about the differing effects of schools on their pupils' academic development have also received a good deal of attention. As he has written: 'Schooling does matter greatly. Moreover, the benefits can be surprisingly long lasting. Schools are about social experiences as well as scholastic learning' (Rutter, 1991). The significance of this study for the concerns discussed here, however, relates to its implications for young people's wellbeing. It showed that differences between schools in outcome were 'systematically related to their characteristics as *social institutions*' (1979: 178, our emphasis). The study emphasised the part schools could play both as environments for learning and as arenas for social development. 'Factors as varied as the degree of academic emphasis, teacher actions in lessons, the availability of incentives and rewards, good conditions for pupils, and the extent to which children were able to take responsibility, were all significantly associated with outcome differences between schools'. As we shall show, there are echoes of these conclusions about schools as social institutions in our review.

Regrettably, there has been a major gap in the research since then. Almost all the studies have focused on *academic* outcomes - wellbeing has been largely ignored despite Rutter drawing attention early on to its significance. The jury is still out, for example, on the question of whether schools which do well in relation to cognitive outcomes do equally well in relation to non-cognitive ones as well (Gray, 2004); the later research shows conflicting patterns. Consequently, whilst the school effectiveness research tradition provides a way of thinking about the area of wellbeing, it still provides relatively few answers.

There are essentially two versions in circulation of how schools might make a difference to adolescents' wellbeing and mental health. The first of these is a good deal more prevalent than the second. In this version, most of the variation in outcomes is assumed to lie between schools. In other words some schools appear to produce better wellbeing outcomes than others – some have problems whilst others do not. The second version notes that most of the variation in outcomes lies within schools rather than between them. In every (or virtually every) school some pupils have better wellbeing outcomes than others – in short, most schools face challenges.

The size of the 'school effect'

We have only been able to identify some half a dozen studies within the school effectiveness tradition that fulfilled three conditions. First, that they related broadly to the age-group we have been interested in. Second, that they included measures of wellbeing in their assessment of outcomes. And third, and importantly, that they provided some empirical estimate of the extent of school differences typically using the statistical method known as multilevel modelling.

The lowest estimate, in this small sample of studies, of the size of school differences is provided by a Finnish study by Konu and colleagues (2002). They report that only 1% of the total variation on their General Subjective Wellbeing indicator was attributable to the school level. A similarly low estimate is provided by Roeger and colleagues (2001: 134) in their study of Australian schools. They comment that they found 'statistically significant school effects on students' depressive symptomatology but that these were smaller than expected; nearly all of the variation (in depressive scores) was present at the student level'. Modin and Ostberg (2009) found similarly low variation between schools in their study of students' psychosomatic complaints. They attributed just 2.5% of the total variation to 'contextual (school) conditions'.

Torsheim and Wold (2001) report similarly low levels of between school variation in outcomes amongst a sample of Norwegian schoolchildren; this amounted to just over 2% of the total individual variance in health complaints. However, they did note large variations between classes within the same school although the sources of this variation are not completely clear.

Three further studies provide slightly higher estimates. Maes and Lievens (2003) reported around 4% school level variance in their study of health behaviours in Belgian (Flemish) schools whilst Smyth (1999) found similar levels of school variance in Irish schools reporting figures of around 5% for measures of stress. Torsheim and Wold (2001: 701), meanwhile, comment that their 'multilevel analysis revealed that the level of health complaints varied across (Norwegian) schoolclasses', estimating that around 5-6% of the variance was at school level. A review of a number of multilevel studies by Sellstrom and Bremberg (2006: 152) draws similar conclusions: 'In four studies on pupils' problem behaviour and wellbeing, the (school variance) did not exceed 8%.. ..... .Health-related behaviours such as physical exercise, smoking and alcohol use seemed to vary between schools to a greater extent than did pupils' problem behaviours and wellbeing'.

The highest estimates of school variance in relation to wellbeing issues come from Opdenakker and Van Damme's (2000) study of Belgian (Flemish) schools. They estimate between school variance from 5% to 11% depending on the particular outcome under consideration but their most interesting finding is possibly in relation to the relationships between cognitive and non-cognitive outcomes. Rutter and Maughan (2002: 462) had earlier concluded in their review of the evidence that 'school-based variations in these emotional/behavioural outcomes (were) far less marked than variations in academic attainments and effects on disruptive behaviours may be stronger than those on indicators of emotional disturbance. Opdenakker and Van Damme concur, concluding that 'schools and classes in Flanders have, like schools in other countries, relatively more influence on achievement than on wellbeing' (*op. cit*: 187). But it is their final conclusion which is perhaps more compelling. 'Our results', they suggest, 'indicate that pupil achievement and wellbeing can be considered as two different, distinctive school and class outcomes'. Whether further research will support this conclusion remains to be seen.

In fact, little of the available evidence is based directly on UK schools and direct evidence on the impact for the 10-14 age-group is largely missing. The research is broadly consistent with that outlined above. Gutman and Feinstein's study of English primary schools (2008: 2) reports that school factors explained 3% or less of the variation in pupils' mental health and behaviour in their sample. They contrast this with the 7% of the variation in Key Stage 2 scores in Maths (at age 11) amongst the same sample and the 10% of variation in KS2 English scores. Their explanation of how schools make a difference to children's wellbeing stresses that it is 'children's individual experiences within schools' which are important. Different children, they argue, experience a very different environment even within the same school, based on their own individual interactions with peers and teachers. And they conclude that 'child-school fit may be more important for children's wellbeing than attending a particular school'. They add, however, that 'much of the variation in children's wellbeing remains unexplained'.

In short, such evidence as we have suggests that the second version of the 'school effect' outlined above may be a better description of the patterns of outcomes than the first – most schools have pupils whose wellbeing outcomes vary widely. Interpretation is made more difficult, however, by the tendency (albeit just a tendency) for more 'resilient' pupils to attend schools which offer greater support. This confounding influence complicates the problem of disentangling cause and effect.

Potentially influential school factors

The sources of the estimated differences in school effectiveness are also of interest. Unfortunately, the picture thrown up by the small number of studies currently available is patchy. Each of the studies considered above had a different focus and measured different aspects of school policies and practices. Consequently it is difficult to draw any firm conclusions from these in isolation although the general direction of the findings is in line with those outlined earlier.

Modin and Ostberg (2009: 445), for example, report that: 'Students who reported that their opinions are taken seriously, that their teachers give praise, that most of their teachers provided interesting teaching, and that they can get immediate help with their schoolwork if needed, had significantly better health than students who did not fully agree with these statements'. But, importantly for this argument, they go on to argue that 'two of the six investigated class-contextual measures displayed a significant relationship with student health over and above those found at individual level. These were classes where a high proportion of students reported that they can get immediate help with their schoolwork and classes with a high prevalence of students reporting that they had been subjected to harassment during the year'. It will be immediately obvious, however, that the factors revealed at school level are considerably fewer than those that showed at the individual level.

Opendakker and Van Damme (2000: 185) draw particular attention to aspects of pupil-teacher relationships. Their study, they argue, 'reveals an overwhelmingly positive effect of teaching staff co-operation in relation to teaching methods and pupil counselling on both (academic) achievement and several wellbeing indicators'. In similar vein Karvonen and colleagues (2005: 436) concluded that 'insufficient support from teachers' was a contextual factor that stood out as particularly detrimental to student health. Meanwhile, Samdal and colleagues (1998: 395) report that 'the most important predictors of the students' satisfaction with school are that the students feel that they are fairly treated, that they feel safe and that they experience teachers that are supportive'.

Other researchers within the effectiveness tradition have also considered a range of school structure and policy variables but with only limited and generally disappointing results. Maes and Lievens (2003: 517), for example, found that 'only a few' of those they considered were 'found to influence the health and risk behaviours of young people', remarking that their 'analysis only partially confirms the hypothesis that the school has an impact on the health behaviour of young people' and concluding that they had 'found few elements in the school contexts that (had) a significant impact'.

Conclusions

Three conclusions may be drawn from the very limited research currently available on the question of school effectiveness and its relationship to wellbeing outcomes. First, the school effect on wellbeing outcomes appears to be quite small and certainly a good deal smaller than schools' probable effects on academic outcomes; most of the variation in wellbeing outcomes seems to lie within individual schools rather than between them. Second, there does not seem to be a strong link between these two different sets of outcomes; schools which do well with respect to boosting pupils' academic achievements will not necessarily do well with respect to nurturing their wellbeing and vice versa. Some studies suggest that there is some overlap but others disagree. For the moment it would seem sensible to see them as separate realms of activity. If synergies can be secured between them, so much the better. Third, and finally, the evidence about what precisely it is about schools' policies and practices that 'makes a difference' to wellbeing outcomes is rather patchy. In the earlier chapter on 'The Supportive School' we argued for the importance of five areas: relationships with teachers, relationships with peers, pupil satisfaction with school, membership of the learning community and the importance of 'thinking small' developments. Such factors appear in the school effectiveness research but, in many cases, exactly how they map onto more favourable wellbeing outcomes for pupils will need to await further research.

CHAPTER TEN

SOME UNANSWERED QUESTIONS

It is widely acknowledged that school factors are not the only (nor necessarily the strongest) influences upon young people's development - peers, neighbourhoods and, crucially, families are also implicated. Each area probably exerts its own independent influence as well as in combination with the others.

Unpicking the school's influence

In Figure 13 below we have attempted to summarise the thinking we have encountered about how these various influences interact. The vertical axis hypothesises the relative contribution of the different areas which are expected to sum to one hundred percent. The figure suggests that influences connected with young people's families and individual circumstances are dominant. It also attributes influence to neighbourhoods, peers and schools although it will be noted that, relative to that suggested for families, we judge the component uniquely associated with schools to be fairly small. Furthermore, in this particular example, we postulate that the relative influence of these different factors remains stable over time; in other words the suggested contribution of the school to the wellbeing of ten-year olds is the same as that for fourteen year-olds and in both instances fairly small.

Figure 14 outlines other possible scenarios. All are variants on the suggestion that, as adolescents develop, they become increasingly influenced by extra-family factors. In the first case (top left) the size of the school component stays relatively constant whilst peer and neighbourhood influences develop in importance, largely at the expense of family and background factors. The second (top right) postulates that all three extra-family factors, including the school, grow in importance over time. The third (bottom left), meanwhile, suggests that, whilst extra-family factors generally increase in influence, the strength of these influences fluctuates over time. Around the age of 11 (when most pupils transfer to secondary school) and, again, around the age of 14, extra-family factors assume additional influence. Other scenarios beyond the four outlined here can also be contemplated.

Figure 13: Relative Influence of Families, Peers, Neighbourhoods and Schools

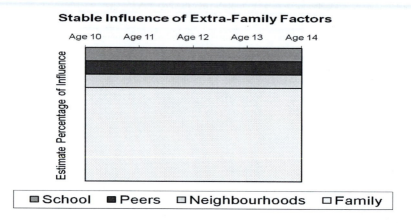

Unfortunately, whilst several potential data-bases exist that could facilitate investigation, at the time of writing we have not been able to identify any analyses which allow us to distinguish with any great certainty (and in an empirical way) between these four alternatives. Our reading of the available evidence, however, inclines us towards one or more of the scenarios which postulate, as young people get older, the declining influence of family background and circumstances. In all of these scenarios the school continues to exert an important influence on wellbeing outcomes.

This strategy for separating out the various strands of influence on adolescents, and then estimating the unique or independent variance associated with each, may under-estimate the contribution of the school. Clearly school influences interact with peer influences and peer influences, in turn, interact with neighbourhood factors. There is also likely to be some interaction between neighbourhood and school as well. Whilst the independent influence of each of the three may be relatively modest, in combination it might be anticipated that they would add more.

Figure 14: Alternative Views of the Relative Influence of Families, Peers, Neighbourhoods and Schools on Wellbeing

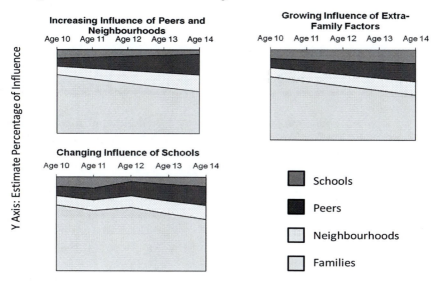

Extending the research on transfer

Transfer from one institution to the next carries risks for adolescents' mental health. The need for schools to think longer-term in relation to transfer is supported by work in other disciplines. For example, in the field of occupational psychology Nicholson (1987) has proposed that work-role transitions consist of four phases. Phase 1, described as *preparation*, parallels the kinds of programme most secondary schools now offer with induction days, visits of the Year 7 tutor to the primary feeder schools, and parents' evenings. This might be extended, as some schools are doing, by increasing the number of induction days to include more experience of typical teaching and by extending the buddy system whereby Year 7 pupils exchange information with their Year 6 peers on a regular basis using forms of communication such as e-mail.

Nicholson's Phase 2 consists of initial *encounters* and would correspond to a post-induction programme which would extend beyond the existing use of activities, such as bridging units, aimed at improving continuity, and include various activities that build on the idea of *'learning to be a professional pupil'* (Lahelma & Gordon, 1997). At the current time only a few schools in England appear to have developed such programmes which include the development of study and thinking skills designed to support independent working, together with the introduction of more cooperative forms of learning and various familiarisation and sensitivity exercises which build on the experiences of earlier schooling. Galton *et al.* (2003) however found that even where these programmes existed they tended to be undertaken in PSHE time and, as a result, the skills learned were not applied in subjects such as mathematics and science where attitudes and motivation are often poorest.

Nicholson's final two phases consist of *adjustment* and *stabilisation* respectively. During the adjustment phase normal working conditions pertain but there is frequent and immediate feedback on both success and failure. While teachers do provide feedback it tends to be *corrective* by pointing out errors, demonstrating the correct procedures etc. rather than *informing* whereby pupils' reasoning is explored and strategies for identifying and correcting mistakes identified (Hattie & Timperley, 2007). Neither is the overall picture of the pupil's progress coordinated other than at parents' evenings and in end of term reports. For Nicholson, stabilisation involves future goal setting and appraisal of what is termed 'role evolution'. This should concentrate on addressing those aspects of the pupil's adjustment (whether social, personal or academic) where improvement is required and setting future goals for the following year. Thus attention to the issues surrounding adjustment at transfer needs to extend beyond the present relatively short periods of concern. This would be in accord with the findings of West et al. (2008) who collected pupils' retrospective views of the transfer experience and found that higher levels of concern at transfer were positively correlated with various measures of wellbeing such as depression and self esteem at two later age points (13 and 15). This is likely to have come about because pupils who have concerns at transfer about making friends, getting on with teachers and so on probably experience similar difficulties in the following years.

There are two areas which remain relatively under-researched in relation to transfer. The first of these deals with multiple transitions and the most appropriate age of transfer. To answer this question fully it would be necessary to track a cohort of children from their last year in their 'first' school at around 9 years of age until one year after transfer to high/secondary school at 14 using as a control a matched group of pupils who experienced a single transfer to a secondary school at 11 years of age (the more traditional pattern). As far as we have been able to ascertain, no such longitudinal studies exist.

The second area where more research is needed concerns the ten per cent of pupils who have severe problems of adjustment at transfer. Most of these are likely to have special needs or to have underperformed relative to their assessed potential in the feeder school. These pupils are likely to be male (ILEA 1986; Muldoon 2005; Evangelou *et al.* 2008). Children with learning difficulties, as we reported in an earlier section, worried more about friendships and being bullied and had a greater chance of being victims (McMaugh & Debus, 1999; Evangelou *et al.* 2008). They had, in part as a consequence of these negative feelings, lower self-esteem (Forgan & Vaughn, 2000; Jindal-Snape & Foggie, 2008). Their relationships with teachers were also less successful (Feeney & Best, 1997), perhaps, as Galton and MacBeath (2008) have observed, because these children tend to have less contact with the class teacher, being assigned for the greater part of the lesson to the classroom assistant. Minority ethnic groups also require further study. Having only a small number of children of similar ethnicity undertaking transfer to a particular school increases concerns, including those of bullying and difficulty in maintaining and making friendships, and also result in a higher probability of disengagement (Benner & Graham, 2007). However, Asian children appear less susceptible to a loss of interest in education than other ethnic groups (Graham & Hill, 2003).

Although many schools pay particular attention to these 'at risk' groups by offering several induction days, sending the Special Educational Needs Coordinator (SENCO) on frequent visits to the feeder school and bringing pupils into the transfer school on the day before the full new intake arrives, these activities largely seem designed to solve administrative problems such as ensuring the requisite number of support staff are available (Galton et al., 2003). Pupils with statements of SEN were almost four times more likely to be excluded than the rest of the school population. Faced with this evidence Warnock (2005: 37) concluded that the policy of inclusion needs to be reviewed. She argued that inclusion should mean that all children 'should be included (in) the common educational project,' and not merely 'that they should be included under one roof.' She pointed to the decision to set up specialist SEN schools as the way forward. Studies assessing the wellbeing of pupils who move to these specialist schools in comparison to those transferring to normal state establishments could therefore prove valuable in helping to develop genuinely inclusive policies.

Conclusions

Sizeable gaps in the landscape of research on wellbeing outcomes remain. Areas identified by this review that might merit further attention include: the relative influence of schooling on young people's wellbeing and, especially, the impact of differences in approach between and within schools; the structures of schooling and the effects of transfer at different ages; and the implications of transfer processes for young people with special educational needs as well as others who are 'at risk'.

CHAPTER ELEVEN

LOOKING TO THE FUTURE

This book has considered the impact of young people's educational experiences at school on their sense of wellbeing and other aspects of their mental health. The evidence clearly supports the view that the greater majority in the 10-14 age-group express 'life satisfaction'. These positive feelings are related, in part, to their responses to schooling although the relationships are not necessarily that strong and there are other influences upon them. Nonetheless a significant minority of young adolescents (typically around 10%) have emotional and conduct disorders whilst larger proportions, varying between a fifth and a third (depending on the measure), express reservations about some aspect or other of their school experiences which probably affects their sense of wellbeing.

A range of school factors have been identified in the review as potentially related to young people's sense of wellbeing. As they get older many young people develop a greater sense of detachment from their schools and teachers and, in a small minority of cases, some sense of alienation. Positive feelings about schooling can serve protective purposes, however. Amongst the numerous components that we have considered, those which emerge with considerable frequency include relationships with teachers, relationships with peers and general satisfaction with the educational experience. These all contribute to greater feelings of 'school connectedness'.

The list has been added to recently by concerns to ensure that young people feel they are members of a learning community in which their participation and voice are actively encouraged. Adolescents value signals from their teachers that they are succeeding in their schoolwork along with help in mediating the pressures that such work can create. A variety of structural features of schooling appear to be compatible with an increased sense of wellbeing, the common denominator being that they all, in one way or another, embody some element(s) of 'thinking small'.

Many of these features of schooling have been addressed discretely by researchers up till now and in isolation from each other. We have coined the term 'the supportive school' to give them some greater coherence.

How firmly 'supportive schools' are embedded in the English system is
not clear and, unfortunately, we are not certain what proportion of schools
can be described in such terms at present. Wellbeing outcomes can be hard
to pin down and 'supportiveness' is not a prominent dimension of the
ways in which most schools are currently organized.

The move from primary to secondary school (or the equivalent transfer
in other educational systems) marks a key transition stage. Since it
typically coincides with the onset of adolescence there is a good deal of
debate about whether educational institutions should be structured to
reflect their changing developmental needs. Schools tend to think of the
transfer as a one-off period with a beginning, middle and end. For
adolescents, by contrast, it is a continuous process which involves frequent
adjustment. During this period personal identities, and crucially how those
identities relate to schooling, are renegotiated. There are difficulties here
in disentangling cause and effect; a good deal more is changing during
these years than just young people's experiences of schooling.
Nonetheless, although the move to secondary school is viewed with some
trepidation by many young people, the greater majority seem to make the
transition fairly readily. For a small minority, however, the change of
environment can begin to generate attitudinal, emotional and conduct
problems. Relationships with teachers can become detached, engagement
with peers may deteriorate, and attitudes towards school in general, and
subjects such as maths and science in particular, may become increasingly
strained.

During this period young people with special educational needs appear
especially vulnerable. Low levels of educational attainment, combined
with emotional and conduct problems, interact to compound the likelihood
of difficulties, both in terms of educational achievement and in relation to
wellbeing outcomes. Peer victimisation seems to affect at least one in ten
adolescents. Whilst the percentages of young people who are formally
excluded from school remain tiny, there are considerable pressures on
schools, in a climate of increased accountability, to be seen to be 'doing
well'. The sizeable increase in exclusions that has occurred over the last
two decades suggests that some schools may have become less tolerant of
'difficult' pupils.

A recent review of this field by Swedish researchers reminds us that
young people's academic performance at school and their levels of mental
health and wellbeing are intimately related (Gustafson et al, 2010: 161).
They reinforce the view that early school failure 'can cause marked
internalizing and externalizing mental health problems'; and they too point
out that relations with peers and teachers can serve as a protective factor.

Many of their recommendations consequently relate to the various ways in which schools might mitigate school failure – intervening early over reading difficulties, ensuring the availability of good teaching and on on. The challenge, they argue, is to prevent the development of 'trajectories of failure'. But perhaps their most important recommendation in relation to the final years of the Swedish comprehensive school is to tackle the ways in which it is dominated by exams and grading; many students, they report, perceive these to be the most important sources of stress in the school environment (Frydenberg, 2008). Formal assessment systems can heighten the sense of failure, not just amongst those young people who are actually under-achieving but also amongst those who fear that they might fall short of expectations.

Monitoring of the educational system has concentrated to date almost exclusively on academic achievement. We were able to identify only a handful of studies which tracked changes in attitudinal outcomes over time and their data was typically related to time-spans of a decade or less. Such evidence as we have, however, suggests that attitudes to school have not got worse in recent years and may, in fact, have improved. Adolescents appear to be more positive about various aspects of their educational experiences including how much they like school, how supportive they find their peers and how they believe their teachers rate them in academic terms. However, they continue to worry about the pressures of schoolwork upon them and this sense of pressure increases considerably amongst the older age groups.

The poor showing of England (and the UK more generally) in international comparisons of child wellbeing has provoked comment. A series of analyses involving cross-Channel (Flemish Belgium, Denmark and the Netherlands) and Nordic countries (Finland, Norway and Sweden), however, suggested that their reports of school experiences compared relatively favourably with those of their counterparts. At least in comparative terms they mostly liked school, found their peers kind and helpful and believed that their teachers judged them to be performing well. In one particular respect, however, they did stand out from their peers in other countries – they felt markedly more pressured by their schoolwork.

Compared to the vast amounts of work that have been undertaken on the academic aspects of schools' effectiveness very little has been done on wellbeing outcomes. To date, the 'school effect' on wellbeing outcomes identified by researchers appears to be quite small; most of the variation in wellbeing outcomes seems to lie within individual schools. Schools which do well with respect to boosting pupils' academic achievements will not necessarily do well with respect to nurturing their wellbeing and vice versa. Some studies suggest that there is some overlap but others disagree. Finally, the evidence about what precisely it is about schools' policies and practices that 'makes a difference' to wellbeing outcomes is rather patchy. Mostly it corresponds to the picture of 'The Supportive School' we painted in an earlier chapter. There is, however, a pressing need for further research on the school effect relating to wellbeing outcomes.

Schools, and especially secondary schools, are currently under considerable pressure to give greater attention to issues of wellbeing. Doubtless, many will be considering whether they have appropriate structures in place whilst others will be contemplating whether to launch new interventions. If there is one overriding message from this book, however, it is that the most important factor affecting young people's wellbeing relates to the cultures of support their schools develop and sustain.

REFERENCES

Alexander, R. J. (2000). *Culture and pedagogy: international comparisons in primary education*. Oxford: Blackwell.

Alexander, R. J., Wilcocks, J., & Kinder, K. M. (1989). *Changing Primary Practice*, London: Falmer Press.

Alspaugh, J. W. (1998). Achievement Loss Associatied with the Transition to Middle School and High School, *The Journal of Educational Research, 92*(1), 20-25.

Alspaugh, J. W., & Hartin, R. D. (1995). Transition Effects of School Grade-Level Organization on Student Achievement, *Journal of Research and Development in Education, 28*(3), 145-149.

Angold, A., Weissman, M., John, K., Merikangas, K., Prusoff, B., Wickramaratne, P. Gammon, D and Warner, V. (1987) 'Parent and child reports of depressive symptoms in children at low and high risk of depression', *Journal of Child Psychology and Psychiatry*, 28, 901-915.

Azmitia, M. & Lippman, D. (1999) On the relation of personal experience to early adolescents' reasoning about best friendship deterioration. *Social Development,* 8, 275– 291.

Baird, J., Gunstone, R., Penna, C., Fensham, P. and White, R. (1990) Researching the balance between cognition and affect in science teaching and learning, *Research in Science Education,* 20, 1, 11-20.

Barmby, P., Kind Per, M., & Jones, K. (2008). Examining changing attitudes in secondary school science, *International Journal of Science Education, 30* (8), 1075-1093.

Barclay, J. and Doll, B. (2001) Early prospective studies of high school dropout, *School Psychology Quarterly,* 16, 357- 69

BEDC (1975). *Continuity in education: Junior to secondary.* Birmingham: City of Birmingham Education Department.

Benner, A. D., & Graham, S. (2007). Navigating the Transition to Multi-Ethnic Urban High Schools: Changing Ethnic Congruence and Adolescents' School-Related Affect, *Journal of Research on Adolescence, 17*(1), 207–220.

Berndt, T. (1981) The effects of friendship on prosocial intentions and behaviour. *Child Development* 52, 638-643.

Berndt, T. (1982) The features and effects of friendship in early adolescence. *Early Adolescence,* 53, 1447 – 1460.

Berndt, T. J., & Mekos, D. (1995). Adolescents' perceptions of the stressful and desirable aspects of the transition to junior high school, *Journal of Research on Adolescence, 10,* 141-158.

Best, R. (1995) Concepts in pastoral care and PSE, in Best, R., Lang, P., Lodge, C. and Watkins, C. (1995) *Pastoral Care and Personal-Social Education: Entitlement and Provision,* London: Cassell.

Best, R., Jarvis, C. and Ribbins, P. (1983) *Education and Care,* London: Heinemann.

Blatchford, P., Bassett, P., & Brown, P. (2008). *Do low attaining and younger students benefit most from small classes? Results from a systematic observation study of class size effects on pupil classroom engagement and teacher pupil interaction.* Paper presented at the Annual Meeting of the American Educational Research Association, New York.

Blatchford, P., Bassett, P., Brown, P., Koutsoubou, M., Martn, C., Russell, A. and Webster, R. (2009) *Deployment and Impact of Support Staff in Schools* (Results from Strand 2, Wave 2), London University: Institute of Education.

Blackburn, K. (1975) *The Tutor,* London: Heinemann.

Blum, R. and Libbey, H. (2004) School connectedness- strengthening health and education outcomes for teenagers. *Journal of School Health,* 74, 231-2.

Blyth, D., A., Simmons, R., G., & Bush, D. M. (1978). The Transition into Early Adolescence: A Longitudinal Comparison of Youth in Two Educational Contexts. *Sociology of Education, 51,* 149-162.

Blyth, D., A., Simmons, R., G., & Carlton-Ford, S. (1983). The Adjustment of Early Adolescents to School Transitions. *The Journal of Early Adolescence, 3,* 105-120.

Bond, L., Butler, H., Thomas, L., Carlin, J., Glover, S., Bowes, G. & Patton, G. (2007) Social and School Connectedness in Early Secondary School as Predictors of late Teenage Substance Use, Mental Health, and Academic Outcomes. *Journal of Adolescent Health,* 40: 357.

Bond, L., Carlin, J.B, Thomas, L., Rubin, K., and Patton G. (2001) Does bullying, *British Medical Journal,* 323, 480-484.

Bond, L., Patton, G., Glover, S., Carlin J.B., Butler, H., Lyndal Thomas, L. and Bowes, G. (2004) The Gatehouse Project: can a multilevel school intervention affect emotional wellbeing and health risk behaviours? *Journal of Epidemiology and Community Health,* 58, 997-1003.

Booth-LaForce, C., Rubin, K., Rose-Karsnor, L. & Burgess, K. (2005) Attachment and Friendship Predictors of Psychosocial Functioning in Middle Childhood and the Mediating Roles of Social Support and Self-Worth. In K. Kerns & R. Richardson (Eds.) *Attachment in Middle Childhood.* New York, Guildford Press.

Bosacki, S. & Wilde Astington, J. (1999) Theory of Mind in Preadolescence: Relations Between Social Understanding and Social Competence. *Social Development*, 8, 2 ,237 – 255.

Boulton, M. and Underwood, K. (1992) Bully/victim problems amongst middle school children, *British Journal of Educational Psychology*, 62, 73-83.

Bowen, N. and Bowen, G. (1998) The effects of home micro system risk factors and school micro system protective factors ion student academic performance and affective investment in schooling. *Social Work in Education*, 20, 219-231.

Bowlby, J. (1969) *Attachment and Loss.* Volume 1. London Hogarth Press

—. (1979) *The Making and Breaking of Affectional Bonds.* London, Routledge.

Boyle, B., Nelson, N. et al. (2000). *Transition from year 6 to year 7 in England: progression or regression?* Manchester: Centre for Formative Assessment, University of Manchester.

BMA (2003) *Housing and Health: building for the future*, London: British Medical Association.

Bradshaw, J., Kemp, P., Baldwin, S. and Rowe, A. (2004) *The Drivers of Social Exclusion: a review of the literature for the Social Exclusion Unit in the Breaking the Cycle series*, London: Social Exclusion Unit, Office of the Deputy Prime Minister.

Brophy J. (1999) towards a model of the value aspects of motivation in education: developing appreciation for particular learning domains and activities. *Educational Psychologist, 34 (2)*, 75-85.

Brown, J., & Armstrong, M. (1986). Transfer from primary to secondary: The child's perspective. In M.Youngman (Ed.), *Mid-Schooling Transfer: Problems and Proposals*, Windsor: NFER-Nelson.

Brown, S. A. (1976). *Affecting objectives in an integrated science curriculum.* PhD Thesis, University of Stirling.

Barclay, J. and Doll, B. (2001) Early prospective studies of high school dropout, *School Psychology Quarterly,* 16, 357- 69.

Buhrmester, D. (1990) Intimacy of Friendship, Interpersonal Competence, and Adjustment during Preadolescence and Adolescence. *Child Development,* 61, 1101-1111.

Buhrmester D. and Prager, K. (1995) Patterns and functions of self-disclosure during childhood and adolescence. In Rotenberg, K. (Ed) *Disclosure processes in children and adolescents.* New York. Cambridge University Press.

CACE. (1967). *Children and Their Primary Schools.* London: Her Majesty's Stationary Office.

Cantin, S., & Boivin, M. (2004). Change and stability in children's social network and self-perceptions during transition from elementary to junior high school, *International Journal of Behavioral Development,* 28(6), 561-570.

Catalano, R., Kostelman, R., Hawkins, J. (1996) Modeling the Etiology of Adolescent Substance Use: A Test of the Social Development Model, *Journal of Drug Issues,* 26(2): 429–455.

Caulfield, C., Hill, M., & Shelton, A. (2005). *The Transition to Secondary School: The Experiences of Black and Minority Ethnic Young People.* Glasgow.

Chedzoy S. M., & Burden, R. L. (2005). Making the Move: Assessing student attitudes to primary-secondary transfer'. *Research in Education,* 74, 22-35.

Child Poverty Action Group (2009) *Child Wellbeing and Child Poverty: Where the UK stands in the European table,* London: Child Poverty Action Group.

Chitty, C. (2002) *Understanding Schools and Schooling,* London: RoutledgeFalmer.

Chung, H., Elias, M., & Schneider, K. (1998). Patterns of Individual Adjustment Changes During Middle School Transition. *Journal of School Psychology,* 36(1), 83-101.

Cohen, J. (1988). *Statistical Power Analysis for the Behavioral Sciences.* Hillsdale, New Jersey: Lawrence Erlbaum Associates.

Coleman, J. C. and Hendry, L.B. (1999) (3rd Edition) *The Nature of Adolescence.* London: Routledge.

Coleman, J.S. et al (1966) *Equality of Educational Opportunity,* Washington DC: US Office of Education, Government Printing Office.

Collishaw, S., Maughan, B., Goodman, R. and Pickles, A. (2004), Time trends in adolescent mental health, *Journal of Child Psychology and Psychiatry,* 45, 1350-1362.

Cook, T., Habib, F., Phillips, M., Settersten, R., Shagie, S. and Degirmencioglu, S. (1999) 'Comer's School Development Program in Prince George's County, Maryland: a theory-based evaluation', *American Educational Research Journal,* 36, 3, 543-597.

Conners, D. A. (1983). The School Environment: A Link to Understanding Stress. *Theory into Practice, 22*(1), 15-20.

Cooper, P., Drummond, MJ., Hart, S., Lovey, J., and McLaughlin, C. (2000) *Positive Alternatives to Exclusion.* London: Routledge.

Cotterell, J. (1986). The adjustment of early adolescent youngsters to secondary school: Some Australian findings. In M. B. Youngman (Ed.), *Mid-Schooling Transfer: Problems and Proposals.* Philadelphia: NfER-Nelson.

—. (1996) *Social Networks and Social Influences in Adolescence,* London, Routledge.

—. (2007) *Social Networks in Youth and Adolescence,* Hove, East Sussex, Routledge.

Cotterell, J. L. (1982). Student Experiences Following Entry into Secondary School. *Educational Research, 24*(4), 297-302.

Covington, M.V. (1992). *Making the Grade.* Cambridge: Cambridge University Press.

Cowie, H. (1998) Perspectives of Teachers and Pupils on the Experience of Peer Support Against Bullying. *Educational Research and Evaluation,* 4, 108-125.

—. (1999) Peers helping peers: interventions, initiatives and insights. *Journal of Adolescence,* 22, 433-436.

Cox, S., Kennedy, S., Bishop, F., & Porteners, S. (2005). *A Study of Students' Transition from Primary to Secondary Schooling: A Work in Progress.*

Craig, W. (1998) The relationships amongst bullying, victimisation, depression, anxiety and aggression in elementary school children, *Personality and Individual Differences*, 24, 123-130.

Craig, W. and Harel, Y. (2004), Bullying, physical fighting and victimization, in Currie, C. et al (eds.)(2004) *Young People's Health in Context: Health Behaviour in School-aged Children: international report from the 2001/2002 survey*, Copenhagen: World Health Organisation Regional Office for Europe.

Crockett, L. J., Petersen, A. C., Graber, J. A., Schuleners, J. E., & Ebata, A. (1989). School transitions and adjustments during early adolescence. *Journal of Early Adolescence, 9*(181-210).

Croll, P. and Moses, D. (2003) Young People's Attitudes to School and their Trajectories into Post-compulsory Education: a preliminary analysis of data from the British Household Panel Survey, Reading University: Institute of Education.

Croxford, L. (2007) Young people's experience of compulsory schooling in England and Scotland during two decades of educational reform, in

G. Bhatti, C. Gaine, F. Gobbo and Y. Leeman (eds) *Social Justice and Intercultural Education*, Stoke on Trent: Trentham Books.

Croxford, L., Iannelli, C., Shapira, M., Howieson, C. and Raffe, D. (2006) *Education and Youth Transitions across Britain 1984-2002*, Briefing no. 39, CES: Edinburgh University.

Csikszentmihalyi, M. and Nakamura, J. (1998) The dynamics of intrinsic motivation: a study of adolescents. In C. Ames and R. Ames (Eds.) *Research on motivation education: goals and cognitions (pp.45-71)* New York: Academic Press.

Csikszentmihalyi, M., Larson, R. & Prescott, S. (1977) The ecology of adolescent activity and experience. *Journal of Youth and Adolescence*, 6, 281-294.

Currie, C. et al (2000) *Health and Health Behaviour Among Young People*, WHO Policy Series: Health Policy for Children and Adolescents, Issue 1, Copenhagen WHO Regional Office for Europe.

Currie, C., Gabainn, S., Godeau, E., Roberts, C., Smith, R., Currie, D., Picket, W., Richter, M., Morgan, A. and Barnekow, V. (eds.)(2008) *Inequalities in Young People's health: HBSC International Report from the 2005/2006 survey*, Copenhagen: World Health Organisation Regional Office for Europe.

Currie, C., Roberts, C., Morgan, A., Smith, R., Settertobulte, W., Samdal, O. and Barnekow Rasmussen, V. (eds.)(2004) *Young People's Health in Context: Health Behaviour in School-aged Children: international report from the 2001/2002 survey*, Copenhagen: World Health Organisation Regional Office for Europe.

Deci, E. L. (1991) The relation of interest to the motivation of behaviour: a self-determination theory perspective. In K.A. Renninger, S. Hidi and A. Krapp (Eds.) *The role of interest in learning and development*, (pp. 43-70) Hillsdale, NJ: Ehrlbaum.

DEFRA (2007) *Survey of Public Attitudes and Behaviours Toward the Environment: 2007*, BMRB report for DEFRA: London.

DCSF. (2008). *Pupil Characteristics and Class Sizes in Maintained Schools in England*. Statistical First Release.London.

Department for Education and Skills (2003) *Every Child Matters.* London: HMSO.

Department of Health (2004) *National service framework for children, young people and maternity services: the mental health and psychological wellbeing of young people*. London: HMSO.

Design Council (2005). *Learning Environments Campaign Prospectus, From the Inside Looking Out*. www.designcouncil.org.

Doherty, J., & Dawe, J. (1985). The relationship between development maturity and attitude to school science: an exploratory study. *Educational Studies, 11*(2), 93-107.

Doll, B. and Hess, R. (2001) Through a new lens: contemporary psychological perspectives on school completion and dropping out of high school. *School Psychology Quarterly,* 16, 351-6.

Dolmans, D. H. J. M., & Schmidt, H. G. (2006). What Do We Know About Cognitive and Motivational Effects of Small Group Tutorials in Problem-Based Learning? *Advances in Health Sciences Education, 11*(1), 321-336.

Douvan, E. & Adelson, J. (1966) *The adolescent experience,* New York, Wiley.

Dunn, J. & Cutting, A. (1999) Understanding Others, and Individual Differences in Friendship Interactions in Young Children. *Social Development,* 8, 201-19.

Dunn, J. (1996) Children's relationships: Bridging the divide between cognitive and social development *Journal of Child Psychology and Psychiatry,* 37, 507-518.

—. (2004) *Children's Friendships: the Beginnings of Intimacy,* Oxford: Blackwell.

Dunn, J., Brown, J. & Beardsall, L. (1991) Family talk about emotions, and children's later understanding of others' emotions. *Developmental Psychology,* 27, 448-55.

Durlak, JA. and Wells, A.M. (1997) Primary Prevention Mental Health Programs for Children and Adolescents: A Meta-Analytic Review, *American Journal of Community Psychology,* 25, 2, 115-152.

Dutch, R., & McCall, J. (1974). Transition to Secondary - An Experiment in a Scottish Comprehensive School. *British Journal of Educational Psychology, 44*(3), 282-289.

Dweck, C. (1986). Motivational Processes Affecting Learning. *American Psychologist, 41*(10), 1040-1048.

Eccles, J. S., Wigfield, A., Flanagan, C. A., Miller, C., Reuman, D. A., & Yee, D. (1989). Self-Concepts, Domain Values, and Self-Esteem: Relations and Changes at Early Adolescence. *Journal of Personality, 57*(2), 283-310.

Eccles, J., & Midgley, C. (1989). Stage/Environment Fit: Developmentally Appropriate Classrooms for Young Adolescents. In R. E. Ames & C. Ames (Eds.), *Research on Motivation and Education: Goals and Cognitions,* (Vol. 3). New York: Academic Press.

Eccles, J., Midgley, C., & Adler, T. F. (1984). Grade-Related Changes in the School Environment: Effects on Achievement Motivation. In J.

Nicholls (Ed.), *The development of achievement motivation*, Vol. 3). Greenwich, CT: JAI Press.

Eccles, J., Midgley, C., Wigfield, A., Reuman, D., Mac Iver, D., & Feldlaufer, H. (1991). Are junior high schools undermining the academic motivation of early adolescents? *Elementary School Journal,* 1-48.

Eccles, J., Early, D., Frasier, K. and Belansky, E. (1997) The Relation of Connection, Regulation, and Support for Autonomy to Adolescents' Functioning. *Journal of Adolescent Research,* 12, 263-286.

Evangelou, M., Taggart, B., Sylva, K., Melhuish, E., Sammons, P., & Siraj-Blatchford, I. (2008). *What Makes a Successful Transition from Primary to Secondary School?* . London: DCSF.

Ehly, S. & Vasquez, E. (1998) Peer Counselling, in Topping, R. & Ehly, S. (Eds) *Peer Assisted Learning* (pp 219-233) Marwah, NJ, LEA.

Farrington, D. (1993) Understanding and preventing bullying, in M. Tonry and N. Morris (eds.) *Crime and Justice*, 17, 381-458, University of Chicago Press.

Feeney, C., & Best, G. F. (1997). Transition of integrated Students and Students with Special Needs from Primary to Secondary School. *Australasian Journal of Special Education, 21*, 36-44.

Fenzel, M. L. (2000). Prospective Study of Changes in Global Self-Worth and Strain During the Transition to Middle School. *The Journal of Early Adolescence, 20*, 93 - 116.

Felner, R., Favazzaa, A., Shim, M., Brand, S., Gu, K. and Noonan, N. (2001), Whole school improvement and restructuring as prevention and promotion: lessons from STEP and the Project on High Performance Learning Communities, *Journal of School Psychology*, 39, 2, 177-202.

Fielding, M., Elliott, J., Burton, C., Robinson, C., & Samuels, J. (2006). *LESS IS MORE? The Development of a Schools-within-Schools Approach to Education on a Human Scale at Bishops Park College, Clacton, Essex*: Department for Education and Skills .

Finn, JD. (1993) *School Engagement and Students at Risk*, Washington; National Center for Education Statistics.

—. (1997) Academic success among students at risk for school failure. *Journal of Applied Psychology.* 82(2):221-34

Forgan, J. W., & Vaughn, S. (2000). Adolescents With and Without LD Make the Transition to Middle School. *Journal of Learning Disabilities, 33*(1), 33-42.

Francis, L., & Greer, J. (1999). Attitudes towards Science among Secondary School Pupils in Northern Ireland: relationship with sex, age and religion. *Research in Science & Technological Education,* *17*(1), 67-74.

Frydenberg, E. (2008) *Adolescent Coping: advances in theory, research and practice,* London: Routledge.

Galton, M., & MacBeath, J. (2008). *Teachers Under Pressure.* London: SAGE, National Union of Teachers.

Galton, M., & Wilcocks, J. (1983). *Moving from the Primary Classroom.* London: Routledge and Kegan Paul.

Galton, M., Comber, C., & Pell, T. (2002). The Consequences of Transfer for Pupils: Attitudes and Attainment. In L. Hargreaves & M. Galton (Eds.), *Transfer from the Primary Classroom, 20 Years On*, pp. 131-158). London: Routledge Falmer.

Galton, M., Gray, J. and Rudduck, J. (2003) *Progress in the Middle Years of Schooling: Continuities and Discontinuities in Learning*, Research Report RR 443, London: Department for Education and Skills.

Galton, M., Simon, B., & Croll, P. (1980). *Inside the Primary Classroom.* London: Routledge and Kegan Paul.

Garrett, Z., Newman, M., Elbourne, D., Bradley, S., Noden, P., Taylor, J., & West, A. (2004). *Secondary School Size: A Systematic Review.* London: EPPI-Centre, Social Science Research Unit, Institute of Education, University of London.

George, R, (2000) Measuring change in students' attitudes to science over time: An application of latent variable growth modelling, *Journal of Science Education and Technology,* 9 (3) 213-225.

—. (2006) A cross domain analysis of change in students' attitudes towards science and attitudes about the utility of science, *International Journal of Science Education,* 28 (6) 571-589.

Gillison, F., Standage, M., & Skevington, S. (2008). Changes in Quality of Life and Psychological Need Satisfaction Following the Transition to Secondary School. *British Journal of Educational Psychology, 78,* 149-162.

Glover, S., Burns, J., Butler, H. and Patton, G. (1998) Social environments and the emotional wellbeing of young people. *Family Matters,* 49, 11-16

Goodenow, C. (1993) Classroom belonging among early adolescent students: Relationships to motivation and achievement. *Journal of Early Adolescence.* 13 , pp. 21-43.

Goodman, R. (1994) A modified version of the Rutter Parent Questionnaire including extra items on children's strengths: a research note, *Journal of Child Psychology and Psychiatry*, 35, 1483-1494.

Gorard, S. and Smith, E. (2008) The impact of school experiences on students' sense of justice: an international study of student voice, *Orbis Scholae*, 2, 2, 87-104.

Gorwood, B. (1986). *School transfer and curriculum continuity*. London: Croom Helm.

Graham, C., & Hill, M. (2003). *Negotiating the transition to secondary school*. Edinburgh: The SCRE Centre.

Gray, J. (2004) School effectiveness and the 'other outcomes' of schooling: a reassessment of three decades of British research, *Improving Schools*, 7, 2, 185-198.

—. (2005) Is failure inevitable? The recent fate of secondary school reforms intended to alleviate social disadvantage, in A. Heath, J. Ermisch and D. Gallie, (eds.) *Understanding Social Change*, Oxford University Press.

Greenhough, P., Hughes, M., Andrews, J., Goldstein, H., McNess, E., Osborn, M., et al. (2007). *What effect does involving parents in knowledge exchange activities during transfer from Key Stage 2 to Key Stage 3 have on children's attainment and learning dispositions?* . Paper presented at the British Educational Research Association Annual Conference, Institute of Education, University of London, 5-8 September.

Gustafson, J-E. et al (20101) *Schools, Learning and Mental Health: a systematic review,* Stockholm: The Health Committee, The Royal Swedish Academy of Sciences.

Gutman, L. M. and Feinstein, L. (2008) Children's Well-being in Primary School: Pupil and School Effects, London: Department for Children, Schools and Families.

Haladyna, T., & Thomas, G. (1979). The attitudes of elementary school children towards school and subject matters. *Journal of Experimental Education, 48*, 18-23.

Hallinan, P., & Hallinan, P. (1992). Seven into Eight will go: Transition from Primary to Secondary School *Australian Educational and Developmental Psychologist, 9*(2), 30-38.

Hamblin, D. (1978) *The Teacher and Pastoral Care*, Oxford: Basil Blackwell.

Harden, A., Rees, R., Shepherd, J., Brunton, G., Oliver, S. and Oakley, A. (2001) *Young People and Mental Health: A systematic review of research on barriers and facilitators,* London Institute of Education: EPPI Centre.

Hargreaves, A., & Tickle, L. (1980). *Middle Schools: origins, ideology and practice*. London: Harper & Row.

Hargreaves, L., & Galton, M. (2002). *Transfer from the Primary Classroom: 20 Years On*. London: RoutledgeFalmer.

Harlen, W. and Deakin-Crick, R. (2002) *A Systematic Review of the Impact of Summative Assessment and Tests on Students' Motivation for Learning*, EPPI-Centre, London Institute for Education.

Hartup, W. and AbecassisM. (2004) Friends and enemies, in P. Smith and C. Hart (eds) *Handbook of Childhood Social Development*, London: Blackwell.

Hattie, J., & Timperley, H. (2007). The Power of Feedback. *Review of Educational Research, 77*(1), 81-112.

Hayden, C. (1997) Exclusion From Primary School: Children 'In Need' And Children With 'Special Educational Needs, *Emotional and Behavioural Difficulties, 2*(3), 36 – 44.

Hirsch, B. J., & Rapkin, B. D. (1987). The Transition to Junior High School: A Longitudinal Study of Self-Esteem, Psychological Symptomatology, School Life, and Social Support. *Child Development, 58*, 1235-1243.

Howard, S., & Johnson, B. (2004). Transition from Primary to Secondary School: Possibilities and Paradoxes. Unpublished paper, aare.edu.an HoW-04184.

Howard, S., Dryden, J. and Johnson, B. (1999) Childhood Resilience: review and critique of literature, *Oxford Review of Education, 25*(3), 307-323.

Hunt, D., E. (1975). Person Environment Interaction: A Challenge Found Wanting Before It Was Tried. *Review of Educational Research, 45*(2), 209-230.

ILEA (1986). *ILEA Transfer Project*. London: Inner London Education Authority.

Institute of Community Health Sciences (2003) *Health of Young People in East London: the Relachs Study 2001*, London: The Stationery Office.

Jennings, K., & Hargreaves, D. J. (1981). Children's Attitudes to Secondary School Transfer. *Educational Studies, 7*(1).

Jindal-Snape, D., & Foggie, J. (2008). A holistic approach to primary–secondary transitions. *Improving Schools, 11*(5), 5-18.

Johnson, B. (2008) Teacher-student relationships which promote resilience at school: a micro level analysis of students' views. *British Journal of Guidance and Counselling, 36*, (4), 385-398.

Johnstone, K. (2002). *The Transition to High School: A Journey of Uncertainty*. Paper presented at the Annual Conference of the Australian Association for Research in Education.

Jones, R. M., & Thornburg, H. D. (1985). The experience of school-transfer: Does previous relocation facilitate the transition from elementary- to middle-level educational environments? . *Journal of Early Adolescence, 5*(2), 229-237.

Juvonen, J. (2007) Reforming Middle Schools: Focus on Continuity, Social Connectedness, and Engagement. *Educational Psychologist, 42*, (4), 197 - 20

Juvonen, J., Le, V-N, Kaganoff, T., Augustine, C. and Constant, L. (2004) *Focus on the Wonder Years: Challenges Facing the American Middle School*, Santa Monica: RAND Corporation.

Kahne, J., Sporte, S., de la Torre, M. and Easton, J. (2008) 'Small high schools on a larger scale: the impact of school conversions in Chicago', *Educational Evaluation and Policy Analysis*, 30, 3, 281-315.

Karvonen, S., Vikat, A. and Rimpela, M. (2005) 'The role of school context in the increase in young people's health complaints in Finland', *Journal of Adolescence*, 28, 1-16.

Konu, A., Lintonen, T. and Autio, V. (2002) 'Evaluation of wellbeing in schools – a multilevel analysis of general subjective wellbeing', *School Effectiveness and School Improvement*, 13, 2, 187-200.

Knuver, A. and Brandsma, H. (1993) 'Cognitive and affective outcomes in school effectiveness research, *School Effectiveness and School Improvement*, 4, 3, 189-204.

Lahelma, E., & Gordon, T. (1997) First day in secondary school: Learning to be a 'professional pupil'. *Educational Research and Evaluation, 3*(2), 119-139.

Lang, P. and Marland, M. (eds) (1986) *New Dimensions in Pastoral Care*, Oxford: Basil Blackwell.

Larson, R. (2002) Globalization, Societal Change, and New Technologies. In Larson, R., Bradford-Brown, B. & Mortimer, J. (Eds.) *Adolescents' Preparation for the Future: Perils and Promise: A report of the study group on adolescence in the twenty-first Century* Arbor, MI.

Larson, R., Richards, M., Moneta, G., Holmbeck, G. & Duckett, E. (1996) Changes in adolescents' daily interactions with their families from ages 10 to 18: Disengagement and transformation. *Developmental Psychology,* 32.744-754.

Layard, R., Dunn, J. and the panel of the Good Childhood Enquiry (2009) *A Good Childhood: Searching for Values in a Competitive Age*, London: Penguin Books.

Lee, V. E., & Burkham, D. T. (2003). Dropping out of High School: The Role of School Organization and Structure. *American Educational Research Journal, 40*(2), 353-393.

Lefstein, A. (2005) Thinking about the technical and the personal in teaching, *Cambridge Journal of Education*, 35, 3, 333-356.

Libbey, H. (2004) Measuring Student Relationships to School: Attachment, Bonding, Connectedness, and Engagement. *Journal of School Health*, 74, 274-82 .

Lightfoot, S.L. (1983) *The Good High School: Portraits of Character and Culture*, New York: Basic Books.

Lipps, G. (2005). *Making the Transition: The Impact of Moving from Elementary to Secondary School on Adolescents' Academic Achievement ad Psychological Adjustment*: Family and Labour Studies Division, Analytical Studies (FaLSDAS) Branch.

Little, S. A., & Garber, J. (2004). Interpersonal and Achievement Orientations and Specific Stressors Predict Depressive and Aggressive Symptoms. *Journal of Adolescent Research, 19*, 63-84.

Longaretti, L. (2006). *School Transition: Aspirations and Inspirations*. Paper presented at the Australian Association for Research on Education.

Louhaus, A., Elben, C. E., Ball, J., & Klein-Hessling, J. (2004). School transition from elementary to secondary school: changes in psychological adjustment. *Educational Psychology 24*(2), 161-173.

Lucey, H., & Reay, D. (2000). Identities in transition: anxiety and excitement in the move to secondary school. *Oxford Review of Education, 26*(2), 191-205.

Maes, L. and Lievens, J. (2003) 'Can the school make a difference? A multilevel analysis of adolescent risk and health behavior', *Social Science and Medicine*, 56, 5-17-529.

Mannarino, A. (1978) Friendship patterns and self-concept development in preadolescent males. *Journal of Genetic Psychology, 133*, 105-110.

—. (1979) The relationship between friendship and altruism in preadolescent girls. *Psychiatry, 42*, 280-284.

Marcus, R. and Sanders-Reio, J. (2001) The influence of attachment on school completion. *School Psychology Quarterly, 16*, 427-44.

Marks, H. (2000) Student Engagement in Instructional Activity: Patterns in the Elementary, Middle, and High School Years. *American Educational Research Journal*, 37 (1), 153-184.

Marland, M. (2002). From 'Form Teacher' to 'Tutor': The Development from the Fifties to the Seventies. *Pastoral Care, 20*(4), 3-11.

Martin, M. O., Mullis, I. V. S., & Foy, P. (2008). *TIMMS 2007 International Science Report: Findings from IEA's Trends in International Mathematics and Science Study at the Fourth and Eighth Grades*. Chestnut Hill, MA: Boston College.

Mayall, B. (2007) Children's Lives Outside School and their Educational Impact. *The Cambridge Primary Review Briefing Report* 8/1, Cambridge.

McLaughlin, C., Arnold, R. and Boyd, E. (2005) Bystanders in schools, *Pastoral Care*, June, 17-22.

McMaugh, A., & Debus, R. (1999). *"Just make friends, that's the most important thing!" School transition and making friends. The concerns and worries of children with illness and disability.* Paper presented at the Annual Conference of the Australian Association for Research in Education.

McNeely, C., Nonnemaber J.M., Blum, R.W. (2002). Promoting school Connectedness: Evidence from the National Longitudinal Study of Adolescent Health. *Journal of School Health,* 72, (4) 138-146.

McNeely, C. and Falci, C. (2004) 'School connectedness and the transition into and out of health-risk behaviour among adolescents: a comparison of social belonging and teacher support, *Journal of School Health*, 74, 7, 284-292.

Measor, L., & Woods, P. (1984). *Changing Schools.* Milton Keynes: Open University Press.

Meltzer, H., Gatward, R. and Ford, T. (1999) *The Mental Health of Children and Adolescents in Great Britain*, London: Office for National Statistics.

Mental Health Foundation (1999) *Bright Future: Promoting Children And Young People's Mental Health,* London: Mental Health Foundation.

Midgley, C & Elelin, K (1998) Middle school reform and early adolescent well-being: The good news and the bad. *Educational Psychologist,* Vol 33, Issue 4, 195-206

Miller, C. L. (1986). *Puberty and Person-Environment Fit in the Classroom.* Paper presented at the Biennial Meeting of the American Educational Research Association, San Francisco.

Miller, D., Parkhouse, P., Eagle, R. and Evans, T. (1999) *Pupils and the Core Subjects: A Study of the Attitudes of Some Pupils Aged 11-16,* Paper presented to the British Educational Research Association (BERA) Annual Conference, University of Sussex at Brighton, September 2-5.

Mitchell, J. V. (1969). Education's Challenge to Psychology: The Prediction of Behavior from Person-Environment Interaction. *Review of Educational Research,* 39, 695-722.

Modin, B. and Ostberg, V. (2009) 'School climate and psychosomatic health: a multilevel analysis', *School Effectiveness and School Improvement*, 20, 4, 433-455.

MORI (2004) *Omnibus Survey of Schools (Wave 10)*, London: MORI.

Mortimore, P., Sammons, P., Stoll, L., Lewis, D. and Ecob, R. (1988) *School Matters: the junior years*, Wells, Somerset: Open Books.

Muldoon, J. (2005). *The significance of teachers and relational change during children's psychological transition to secondary school*. PhD Thesis, University of Lancaster.

Murray, C. and Greenberg, M. (2000) Children's relationship with teachers and bonds with school: an investigation of patterns and correlates in middle childhood. *Journal of School Psychology*, 38(5), 423-445.

Newman, M. (2008). Big or Small: does the size of a secondary school matter? *Forum, 50*(2), 167-176.

Newmann, F. (1992) *Student Engagement and Achievement in American Secondary Schools.* New York: Teachers College Press.

Nicholson, N. (1987). The Transition Cycle: A Conceptual Framework for the Analysis of Change and Human Resources Management. *Research in Personnel and Human Resources Management, 5*, 167-222.

Northern Ireland (2005) *Review of Mental Health and Learning Disability: vision of a comprehensive child and adolescent mental health service*, Northern Ireland: consultation document November 2005.

Nuffield Foundation (2009) *Time Trends in Adolescent Wellbeing (Updated 2009)*, London: Nuffield Foundation.

Office for National Statistics (2003) *The mental health of young people looked after by local authorities in England*, London: HMSO.

—. (2005) *Mental Health in Children and Young People in Great Britain*, London: HMSO.

Ofsted (2004) *Out of School: A survey of the educational support and provision for pupils not in school*, London: Ofsted.

—. (2005) *Pupils' Satisfaction with their School*, London: Ofsted

—. (2007) *TellUs2 National Report*, London: Ofsted.

—. (2007b) *Developing Social, Emotional and Behavioural Skills in Secondary Schools*, London: Ofsted.

—. (2008) *Indicators of a School's Contribution to Wellbeing*, Ofsted consultation document, October 2008.

—. (2008) *TellUs3 National Report*, London: Ofsted.

Olweus, D. (1991) Bully/victim problems among school children, in Pepler, D. and Rubin, K. (eds.) *The Development and Treatment of Childhood Aggression*, Hillsdale: Erlbaum.

—. (1994) Bullying at school: basic facts and the effects of a school-based intervention program, *Journal of Child Psychology and Psychiatry*, 35, 7, 1171-1190.

Opdenakker, M-C. and Van Damme, J. (2000) Effects of schools, teaching staff and classes on achievement and wellbeing in secondary education: similarities and differences between school outcomes, *School Effectiveness and School Improvement,* 11, 2, 165-196.

Osborne, J., Shirley, S., & Collins, S. (2003). Attitudes towards science: a review of the literature and its implications. *International Journal of Science Education, 25*(9), 1049-1079.

Parry-Langdon, N. (2008) *Three Years On: Survey of the Development and Emotional Well-being of Children and Young People,* London: Office for National Statistics.

Parsons, C. (2005) School Exclusion: the Will To Punish, *British Journal of Educational Studies,* 53 (2), 187-211.

Parsons, C., Hayden, C., Godfrey, R., Howlett, K. and Martin, T. (2001) *Outcomes in Secondary Education for Children Excluded from Primary School,* London: DfEE. Research Report 271.

Pell, T., Galton, M., Steward, S., Page, C., & Hargreaves, L. (2007). Promoting group work at key stage 3: solving an attitudinal crisis among young adolescents. *Research Papers in Education, 22*(3), 309-332.

Petersen, A. C., & Crockett, L. J. (1985). Pubertal timing and grade effects on adjustment. *Journal of Youth and Adolescence, 14,* 191-206.

Pietarinen, J. (2000). Transfer to and study at secondary school in Finnish school culture: developing schools on the basis of pupils' experiences. *International Journal of Educational Research, 33*(4), 383-400.

Plowden, Lady (chair)(1967) *Children and their Primary Schools,* London: HMSO.

Pople, L. (2009) *The Good Childhood Inquiry: What Children Told Us,* London: Children's Society.

Power, S. (1996) *The Pastoral and the Academic: Conflict and Contradiction in the Curriculum,* London: Cassell.

Pratt, S., & George, R. (2005). Transferring Friendship: Girls' and Boys' Friendships in the Transition from Primary to Secondary School. *Children and Society, 19*(1), 16-26.

Raffe, D., Croxford, L., Iannelli, C., Shapira, M. and Howieson, C. (2006) Social class inequalities in education in England and Scotland, CES Briefing no. 40, Edinburgh: Centre for Educational Sociology.

Ravens-Sieberer, U., Kokonyei, G. and Thomas, C. (2004) School and Health, in Currie, C., Roberts, C., Morgan, A., Smith, R., Settertobulte, W., Samdal, O. and Barnekow Rasmussen, V. (eds.)(2004) *Young People's Health in Context: Health Behaviour in School-aged Children:*

international report from the 2001/2002 survey, Copenhagen: World Health Organisation Regional Office for Europe.

Reddy, R., Rhodes, J. and Mulhall, P. (2003) The influence of teacher support on student adjustment in the middle school years: a latent growth curve study, *Development and Psychopathology*, 15, 119-138.

Resnick, MD. (2000) Protective factors, resiliency and healthy youth development. *Adolescent Medicine,* 11(1), 157-65.

Resnick, MD., Bearman, PS., Blum, RW. and Bauman, KE. (1997) Protecting adolescents from harm. Findings from the National Longitudinal Study on Adolescent Health. *Journal of the American Medical Association*, 278, 823-32.

Resnick, MD., Harris, LJ. and Blum, RW. (1993) The impact of caring and connectedness on adolescent health and well-being. *Journal of Paediatrics and Child Health,* 29(1), 3-9.

Rigby, K. (2004) Bullying in children, in P. Smith and C. Hart (eds.) *Handbook of Childhood Social Development*, London: Blackwell.

—. (2005) Bullying in Schools and the Mental Health of Children, *Australian Journal of Guidance and Counselling*, 15,(2), 195-208

Roeser, RW., Eccles, JS. and Sameroff, AJ. (2000) School as a context of early adolescents' academic and social-emotional development; a summary of the research findings. *The Elementary School Journal.* 100,5, 443-471.

Rogers, C., Galloway, D., Armstrong, D., Jackson, C., & Leo, E. (1994). Change in Motivational Style over the Transfer from Primary to Secondary School: Subject and Dispositional Effects. *Educational and Child Psychology, 11*(2), 26-38.

Rosenberg, M. (1989) *Society and the Adolescent Self-Image*, Middletown CT: Wesleyan University Press.

Rosenfeld, LB., Richman, JM. and Bowen, GL. (2000) Social Support Networks and School Outcomes: The Centrality of the Teacher. *Child and Adolescent Social Work Journal,* 17, (3), 204-226.

Rudd, P., Reed, F., & Smith, P. (2008). *The effects of the school environment on young people's attitudes towards education and learning*: Slough: National Foundation for Educational Research.

Rudduck, J., Chaplain, R., & Wallace, G. (eds.). (1996). *School improvement: What can pupils tell us?* London: David Fulton.

Rudduck, J. and Flutter, J. (2004) *How to Improve Your School; Giving Pupils a Voice*, London: Continuum.

Rudolph, K. D., Lambert, S. F., Clark, A. G., & Kurlajowsky, K. D. (2001). Negotiating the transition to middle school: the role of self-regulatory processes. *Child Development*, 72(3), 929-946.

Rutter, M. (1991) 'Pathways to and from childhood to adult life: the role of schooling.' *Pastoral Care in Education,* 9 (3), 3-10.

Rutter, M. and Smith, D. (1995) *Psychosocial Disorders in Young People: Time Trends and Their Causes,* Chichester: John Wiley.

Rutter, M., Maughan, B., Mortimore, P. and Ouston, J. (1979), *Fifteen Thousand Hours: Secondary Schools and their Effects on Children,* London: Open Books.

Rutter, M. and Maughan, B. (2002) School effectiveness findings 1979-2002, *Journal of School Psychology,* 40, 6, 451-475.

Samdal, O., Nutbeam, D., Wold, B. and Kannas, L. (1998) Achieving health and educational goals through schools – a study of the importance of the school climate and the students' satisfaction with school, *Health Education Research: Theory and Practice,* 13, 3, 383-397.

Savin-Williams, R. & Berndt, T. (1990) Friendship and peer relations. In Feldman, S. & Elliot, G. (Eds.) *At the threshold: the developing adolescent.* Cambridge MA, Harvard University Press.

Schofield, T. (2007). Student and Tutor Perceptions of the Role of the Tutor in a Sixth Form College. *Pastoral Care in Education,* 25(1), 26-32.

Schools Council (1972) *Education in the Middle Years,* Working paper No 2, London: Evans-Methuen.

Scottish Executive, S. (2007). *Transitions Evaluation.* Edinburgh: Scottish Executive Education Department.

Sebba, J., Brown, N., Steward, S., Galton, M. and James, M. (2007) *An Investigation of Personalised Learning Approaches Used by Schools,* London: DfES.

Seidman, E., LaRue, A., Lawrence, A., J., Mitchell, C., & Fienman, J. (1994). The Impact of School Transitions in Early Adolescence on the Self-System and Perceived Social Context of Poor Urban Youth. *Child Development,* 65(2), 507-522.

Seifert, T., & Schulz, H. (2007). The Effects of Pubertal Timing and School Transition on Preadolescents' Well-Being. *Canadian Journal of School Psychology,* 22, 219-234.

Sellstrom, E. and Bremberg, S. (2006) 'Is there a "school effect" on pupil outcomes? A review of multilevel studies', *Journal of Epidemiology and Community Health,* 60, 149-155.

Shachar, H., Suss, G., & Sharan, S. (2002). Students' concerns about the transition from elementary to junior high school: a comparison of two cities. *Research Papers in Education,* 17(1), 79-95.

Silins, H., & Mulford, B. (2000). *Towards an optimistic future: schools as learning organisations: effects on teacher leadership and student outcomes.* Paper presented at the annual AARE-NZARE Conference, Sydney.

Simmons, R., G., Blyth, D., A., Van Cleave, E. F., & Bush, D. M. (1979). Entry Into Early Adolescence: The Impact of School Structure, Puberty, and Early Dating on Self-Esteem. *American Sociological Review, 44*, 948-967.

Simon, A., & Ward, L. O. (1982). Anxiety, Self-Concept, Attitude to School and Transition to the Comprehensive School. *Counsellor, 3*(5), 33-39.

Simpson, R. D., & Oliver, S. J. (1985). Attitude toward Science and Achievement Motivation Profiles of Male and Female Science Students in Grades Six through Ten. *Science Education, 69*(4), 511-526.

Skinner, E., Marchland, G., Furrer, C. and Kindermann, T. (2008) Engagement and disaffection in the classroom: part of a larger motivational dynamic? *Journal of Educational Psychology*, 100, 4, 765-781.

Smith, D. (2006) 'School Experience and Delinquency at Ages 13 to 16,' *Edinburgh Study of Youth Transitions and Crime, No. 13.* Edinburgh Centre for Law and Society, University of Edinburgh, UK.

Smith, P.K. (2003) *Violence in Schools: the Response in Europe.* London: RoutledgeFalmer.

Smith, F., Hardman, F., Wall, K. and Mroz, M. (2004) Interactive whole class teaching in the National Literacy and Numeracy Strategies, *British Educational Research Journal,* 30 (3): 395-412.

Smith, P. and Sharpe, S. (eds.)(1994) *School Bullying,* London: Routledge.

Smith, P. and Shu, S. (2000) What good schools can do about bullying, *Childhood*, 7, 193-212.

Speering, W., Rennie, & Léonie. (1996). Students' perceptions about science: The impact of transition from primary to secondary school. *Research in Science Education, 26*(3), 283-298.

Spelman, B. J. (1979). *Pupil Adaptation to Secondary School.* Belfast, Northern Ireland: Northern Ireland Council for Educational Research.

Steinberg, L. & Monahan, K. (2007) Age Differences in Resistance to Peer Influence. *Developmental Psychology*, 43, 6, 1531 – 1543.

Steinberg, L. (1996) *Beyond the Classroom: Why school reform has failed and what parents need to do.* New York: Simon and Schuster.

Stirling, M. (1992) How Many Pupils are Being Excluded? *British Journal of Special Education,* 19, (4), 128-30.

—. (1996) Government Policy and Disadvantaged Children, in E. Blyth
and J. Milner (eds.) *Exclusions from School, Inter-professional issues
for Policy and Practice,* London: Routledge.

Suffolk LEA (2001). *Review of Transfer.* Ipswich: Suffolk County
Council.

Suffolk LEA (2006). *School Organisation Review.* Report of the Policy
Development Panel: Ipswich: Suffolk County Council.

Suldo, S. and Huebner, E. (2006) 'Is extremely high life satisfaction
during adolescence advantageous?' *Social Indicators Research,* 78,
179-203.

Summerfield, M. (1986). Academic Performance after Transfer. In M. B.
Youngman , *Mid-Schooling Transfer: Problems and Proposals* (ed.),
pp. 11-28). Slough: NfER-Nelson.

Symonds, J. E. (2007). The Ambiguities of Comparing Transfer 'Effects'
Between Two and Three Tier Systems: suggestions for improving
declines in pupils' attitude and achievement. *The National Middle
Schools Forum,* www.middleschools.org.uk.

Tasker, M. (2008). Smaller Schools: a conflict of aims and purposes?
Forum, 50(2), 177-184.

Teddlie, C. and Reynolds, D. (eds.)(2000) *The International Handbook of
School Effectiveness Research,* London: Falmer Press.

Thompson, D., Iachan, R., Overpeck, M., Ross, J. and Gross, L. (2006)
School connectedness in the Health Behaviour in School-Aged
Children Study: the role of student, school and neighbourhood
characteristics, *Journal of School Health,* 76, 7, 379-386.

TIMMS. *Trends in International Mathematics and Science Study* IES
National Center for Education Statistics: U.S. Department of
Education, Institute of Education Sciences.

Tindall, J. & Gray, H. (1989) *Peer Counselling.* Philadelphia, Research
Press.

Tindall, J. (1995) *Peer programs: an in-depth look at peer helping:
planning, implementation, and administration.* St Charles, MO;
Accelerated Development.

Torsheim, T. and Wold, B. (2001) School-related stress, support, and
subjective health complaints among early adolescents: a multilevel
approach, *Journal of Adolescence,* 24, 701-713.

Turner, J. (1999) Some current issues in research on social identity and
self-categorization theories. In Ellemers, N., Spears, R. & Doosje, B
(Eds) *Social identity: context, commitment, content.* pp. 6-34. Oxford,
Blackwell.

Tymms, P., Bolden, D. and Merrell, C. (2008) Science in English Primary
    Schools: trends in attainment, attitudes and approaches, *Perspectives
    on Education 1 (Primary Science)* 19-43,
    www.welcome.ac.uk/perspectives [accessed 9 January 2009].
Unicef (2007) *An Overview of Child Well-being in Rich Countries: a
    comprehensive assessment of the lives and well-being of children and
    adolescents in the economically advanced nations,* UNICEF, Innocenti
    Research Centre.
Vieno, A., Santinello, M., Galbiati, E and Mirandola, M. (2004) School
    setting, school climate and wellbeing in early adolescence: a
    comprehensive model, *European Journal of School Psychology,* 2, 1,
    219-238.
Voelkl, K. (1995) School warmth, student participation and achievement,
    Journal of Experimental Education, 63, 2, 127-138.
Volk, A. et al ((2006) Adolescent risk correlates of bullying and different
    types of victimization, *International Journal of Adolescent Medicine
    and Health,* 18, 4, 575-86.
Vostanis, P. (2007) Mental health and mental disorders, in J. Coleman and
    A. Hagell (2007) *Adolescence Risk and resilience: against the odds.*
    Chichester: John Wiley.
Ward, R. (2000). Transfer from middle to secondary school: a New
    Zealand study. *International Journal of Educational Research, 33*(3),
    365-374.
Wargo Aikins, J., Bierman, K. L., & Parker, J. G. (2005). Navigating the
    Transition to Junior High School: The Influence of Pre-Transition
    Friendship and Self-System Characteristics. *Social Development,
    14*(1), 42-59.
Warnock, M (2005) *Special Educational Needs: A new look,* Impact No
    11, London: Philosophy of Education Society of Great Britain.
Weare, K. and Gray, G. (2003) *What Works in Developing Children's
    Emotional and Social Wellbeing?* Research Report RR456. London:
    Department for Education and Skills.
Webb, R., & Vulliamy, G. (2006). The impact of New Labour's education
    policy on teachers and teaching at Key Stage 2. *Forum, 48*(2), 145-
    157.
Wells, J., Barlow, J. and Stewart-Brown, S. (2003) A systematic review of
    universal approaches to mental health promotion in schools, *Health
    Education,* 103, 197-220.
Wentzel. K. R. (1998) School Relationships and Motivation in Middle
    School: The Role of Parents, Teachers and Peers. *Journal of
    Educational Psychology,* 90, (2), pp. 202-209.

West, P., Sweeting, H., & Young, R. (2008). Transition matters: pupils' experiences of the primary-secondary school transition in the West of Scotland and consequences for well-being and attainment. *Research Papers in Education*, 1-29.

WHO (2000) Health and Health Behaviour among Young People: International report from the HBSC 1997/98 survey, Copenhagen, WHO Regional Office for Europe.

Wubbels, T. and Levy, J, (1993 *Do You Know What You Look Like?: Interpersonal Relationships In Education*. London: Routledge.

Wyatt, N. (2008) *Middle School Inspection Outcomes: A report on the three year cycle of middle school inspections*, London: National Middle Schools' Forum.

Yager, R. E., & Yager, S. O. (1985). Changes in Perceptions of Science for Third, Seventh, and Eleventh Grade Students. *Journal of Research in Science Teaching*, 22(4), 347-358.

Yecke, C. P. (2005). Mayhem in the middle: How middle schools have failed America - and how to make them work. Thomas B. Fordham Institute: http://www.edexcellence.net/detail/news.cfm?news_id=345.

Youngman, L., & Lunzer, E. (1977). Adjustment to Secondary Schooling: School of Education, University of Nottingham.

Youngman, M. (1978). Six Reactions to School Transfer. *British Journal of Educational Psychology*, 48(4), 282-289.

Zanobini, M., & Usai, C. (2002). Domain specific self-concept and achievement motivation in the transition from primary to low middle school. *Educational Psychology*, 22(2), 203-217.

Zeedyk, M. S., Gallagher, J., Henderson, M., Hope, G., Husband, B., & Lindsay, K. (2003). Negotiating the transition from primary to secondary school: perceptions of pupils, parents and teachers. *School Psychology International*, 24, 67-79.

Zimet, G., Dahlem, N., Zimet, S. and Farley, G. (1988) The Multi-Dimensional Scale of Perceived Social Support, *Journal of Personality Assessment*, 52, 30-41.

APPENDIX 1:
THE REVIEW STRATEGY

We adopted two related strategies for the literature search. Questions related to the 'supportive school' were addressed by entering a number of potentially related terms into the major bibliographic search engines (both inside and outside education), paying particular attention to those aspects of social and emotional development and behaviour which previous reviews have linked to schooling. These approaches were also supplemented by more *ad hoc* approaches. The main search terms used either separately or in combination were based around the following themes or variants of them:

Adolescent Mental Health
Friendship in Adolescence
Adolescent mental health in schools
School Connectedness
Pupil-teacher relationships
Bullying in Adolescence
School Preventative Programmes Adolescence
School Effectiveness
School Exclusion
School, emotion, adolescence
School, emotion, attachment
Wellbeing and Schools

We paid particular attention to studies on young adolescents (within the 10-14 age range). We drew on papers in psychology, health, medicine, education and criminology. A total of over 130 papers were identified and reviewed. The majority of these, were from the United States with some from the UK and Australia.

The part of the review relating to school transfer is based on over 200 articles and research reports which were tracked down by similar means to those described above. Nearly half of these were of UK origin with a further third originating in the USA and around ten per cent from Australia and New Zealand. Most of these studies have been concerned to solicit pupils' opinions, self-reported psychology and behaviour before and after transfer either through surveys (around 50%), interviews (12%) or through a combination of both qualitative and quantitative methods (15%). Around 20% of the studies investigated consisted of research reviews. In the UK the majority of the studies covered the move from primary to secondary school at the age of eleven while those in the USA were more widespread and involved transfer from elementary school to middle, junior high and high schools.

Of the various international data-sets we have reviewed we have found the Health Behaviour in School-Aged Children (HBSC) surveys to be the most useful and comprehensive. This study, conducted on behalf of the World Health Organisation, is a network of researchers from around the world brought together at regular intervals to conduct surveys of young people. The studies have been co-ordinated by Prof. Candace Currie, Director of the Child and Adolescent Health Research Unit at the University of Edinburgh, to whom we are extremely grateful for co-operation and support.

There have been four published surveys to date and we have made use of the second, third and fourth which cover the years 1997/98, 2001/02 and 2005/2006 (see Currie et al, 2008 for fuller details). These reports provide a great deal of detailed empirical information summarising the position in each participating country. We have drawn on this summary information to construct some of the tables in this report but clearly a great deal more could be done with this rich resource. The latest survey covered more than 200,000 young people in 41 countries; the English estimates in this particular survey were based on achieved sample sizes of around 4800 pupils.

APPENDIX 2:
STUDIES EMPLOYED IN THE TRANSFER ANALYSES

The studies used in the analysis of pre-and post-transfer perceptions were as listed in the table below.

Reference	Date	Sample Size	Age	Method
UK				
Bryan	1980	310	11.5	Essays
Brown & Armstrong	1986	220	11.5	Essays
Suffolk Local Authority	2001	*	11.5	Survey & Observations
Graham & Hill	2003	268	11.5	Survey
Caulfield et al.	2005	176	11.5	Interviews (retrospective)
Chedzoy & Burden	2005	207	11.5	Survey
Pratt & George	2005	30	11.5	Survey & Interviews
Evangelou et al.	2008	550	11.5	Survey (retrospective)
US				
Berndt & Mekos	1995	101	12.5	Interviews
Europe				
Pietarinen	2000	132	11.5	Essays

Australia & New Zealand				
Johnstone	2002	13	12.5	Interviews & Diaries
Ward	2000	18	13.5	Interviews
	Total	2025+		

* Sample size not given in the reports

A number of issues had to be dealt with in the meta-analysis of psychological measures and in interpreting these data several limitations need to be borne in mind. First, the various instruments employed in different studies to measure a particular characteristic are not always identical. For example, instruments measuring 'liking school', 'school enjoyment' and 'feelings of belonging to the school' have been grouped under the general heading of '*attitude to school*'.

Second, it is only possible to indicate the direction of changes and not the magnitude, since the rating scales used in different studies were not identical.

Third, not all studies carried out measurements at four points in time. Where only two or three points were available between the end of the year in the feeder school and one year after transfer, a 'dummy variable' was created that marked the mid-point between available effect sizes. Some studies had two samples (Galton, Hargreaves & Pell 2003 and Youngman & Lunzer 1977) and both were included as they were different year group cohorts transitioning at different times.

Two unpublished analyses are also used. The first is data from Galton's study of attitudes in Northampton. This is marked with an asterix and dated as 2006 (when the analysis was conducted). Another data set was included through a secondary analysis of the Michigan Study of Adolescent Life Transitions data (gathered in 1983/1984). This was conducted with permission from Jacquelynne Eccles at the University of Michigan and is reported as 'Symonds with Vida and Eccles, 2008'.

The studies used in the analysis of effect sizes (attitudes to school and psychological dispositions) are listed in the table below:

UK

Reference	Date	Sample Size	Age	Data Gathering Time Points					
				Primary School			Secondary School		
				Term1	Term 2	Term 3	Term 1	Term 2	Term 3
Youngman & Lunzer A	1977	290	11.5	✓			✓		
Youngman & Lunzer B	1977	359	11.5	✓			✓		✓
Galton, Comber & Pell	2002	609	11.5	✓			✓		✓
Galton, Hargreaves & Pell A	2003	1,315	11.5	✓		✓	✓		✓
Galton, Hargreaves & Pell B	2003	521	11.5	✓		✓	✓		✓
Galton[1]	2006	71	11.5	✓		✓	✓		✓
		Total 3165	Av. 11.5						

US and Canada

Reference	Date	Sample Size	Age	Data Gathering Time Points					
				Elementary School			Middle School or Junior High School		
				Term1	Term 2	Term 3	Term 1	Term 2	Term 3
Hirsch & Rapkin	1987	159	12.5	✓			✓		✓
Feldlaufer & Midgley	1988	2,210	12.5	✓		✓	✓	✓	✓
Midgley et al.	1989	1,329	12.5	✓		✓	✓		✓
Crockett et al.	1989	181	11.5		✓		✓	✓	
Seidman et al.	1994	863	9-13			✓	✓		✓
Chung et al.	1998	99	11.5			✓	✓		✓
Fenzel	2000	116	11.5			✓	✓	✓	✓
Rudolph et al.	2001	329	11.5			✓	✓		✓

[1] Unpublished data

Appendix 2: Studies Employed in the Transfer Analyses

Study	Year			Junior High School		High School		
				Term 2	Term 3	Term 1	Term 2	Term 3
Cantin & Boivin	2004	142	12.5	✓	✓	✓		✓
Wargo-Aikins et al.	2005	111	12.5		✓	✓	✓	
Symonds with Vida & Eccles	2008	2,263	12.5	✓	✓	✓		✓
Benner & Graham	2007	918	14.5	✓	✓	✓		
		Total	*Av.*					
		8867	12.5					

From these, the studies used in the specific analysis of attitude to school, their measures and their final effect sizes are listed in the following table.

Study		Item or Scale	Final Sample	Cohen's D	Effect Size
UK					
Hargreaves & Galton	2002	Enjoyment of School	281	-0.17	Small
Galton, Hargreaves & Pell A	2003	Attitude to School	1315	-0.06	Negligible
Galton, Hargreaves & Pell B	2003	Attitude to School	521	-0.03	Negligible
Galton	2006	Liking School	70	-0.74	Medium
US					
Hirsch & Rapkin	1987	Satisfaction with School	159	-0.82	Large
Benner & Graham	2007	School Belonging	807	0.01	Negligible
Symonds with Vida & Eccles	2008	I Like School this Year	2263	0.08	Negligible

Further studies were used in the analysis of attitudes to subjects. These were:

- Attitude to Maths (Midgley et al. 1989; Galton, Hargreaves & Pell 2003; Galton 2006; Symonds with Vida & Eccles 2008)
- Attitude to Science (Galton, Hargreaves & Pell 2003; Galton 2006)
- Attitude to English (Galton, Hargreaves & Pell 2003; Galton 2006, Symonds with Vida & Eccles 2008)

The studies employed in the analysis of changes in self-oriented psychology were as follows:

- Academic self concept (Youngman & Lunzer, 1977; Fenzel 2000; Galton, Comber & Pell 2002; Cantin & Boivin, 2004; Symonds with Vida & Eccles 2008)
- Social adaptation (Youngman & Lunzer 1977; Crockett et al. 1989; Seidman et al. 1994; Galton, Hargreaves & Pell 2003; Galton, Comber & Pell 2002; Cantin & Boivin 2004; Wargo-Aikins et al. 2005)
- Motivation (Youngman & Lunzer, 1977; Crockett *et al.*1989; Seidman *et al.*1994; Galton, Comber & Pell 2002; Galton 2006; Symonds with Vida & Eccles 2008).
- School based anxiety (Fenzel, 2000; Rudolph et al., 2001; Benner & Graham, 2007)
- Self esteem (Youngman & Lunzer, 1977; Crockett et al., 1989; Seidman et al., 1994; Chung, Elias, & Schneider, 1998; Galton, Comber & Pell 2002; Cantin & Boivin, 2004)

THE CHANGING ADOLESCENCE RESEARCH PROGRAMME

.

The **Changing Adolescence Programme** was established in 2005 by the Nuffield Foundation, based in London, in response to research findings that showed a significant increase in young people's emotional and behavioural problems between 1975 and 1999.

The main aim of the programme was to examine the reasons for these increases and to better understand how the lives of young people have changed over the last 30 or so years.

The programme consisted of a series of commissioned research reviews, of which this book was one, designed to look at various aspects of teenage life as well as any evidence of emerging trends over time. At the same time a number of seminars and workshops were held to bring together researchers, policy makers and practitioners in strategic discussions.

Specific projects were commissioned on the following topics related to adolescent development:

- Time trends in adolescent wellbeing
- Parenting
- How young people spend their time
- Drugs and alcohol misuse
- Neighbourhoods, schools and families
- Young people and stress
- School experience.

The research programme was chaired for the Nuffield Foundation by Professor Sir Michael Rutter and co-ordinated by Dr. Ann Hagell.

Further details about the research, as well as updated information about other publications emerging from the various projects, can be found at the following address: www.nuffieldfoundation.org/changing-adolescence.

A book about the whole Changing Adolescence Research Programme, edited by Ann Hagell, will be published by Policy Press in 2012 entitled *Changing Adolescence: Social Change and Adolescent Mental Health.*

AUTHOR AND SUBJECT INDEX